PRECEPTS
FOR
LIVING®

PERSONAL STUDY GUIDE

UMI MISSION STATEMENT

*We are called
of God to create, produce, and distribute
quality Christian education products;
to deliver exemplary customer service;
and to provide quality Christian
educational services, which will empower
God's people, especially within the Black
community, to evangelize, disciple,
and equip people for serving Christ,
His kingdom, and church.*

Precepts For Living® Personal Study Guide, Vol. 14, September 2014–August 2015. Published yearly by UMI (Urban Ministries, Inc.), P.O. Box 436987, Chicago, IL 60643-6987. Founder and Chairman: Melvin E. Banks Sr., Litt.D.; CEO: C. Jeffrey Wright, J.D.; Senior Editor: Dr. A. Okechukwu Ogbonnaya, Ph.D.; Associate Director of Adult Content Development: John C. Richards, Jr., M.Div., J.D.; Editors/Writers: Ramon Mayo, M.A.; Beth Potterveld, M.A.; Designer: Lolita Westbrook. Lessons based on International Sunday School Lessons; the International Bible Lessons for Christian Teaching. Copyright © 2010 by the Committee on the Uniform Series. Used by permission. Supplementary Lesson Development. Copyright © 2014 by UMI. All rights reserved. $7.95 per copy. Printed in the U.S.A. **NO PART OF THIS PUBLICATION MAY BE REPRODUCED IN ANY FORM WITHOUT THE WRITTEN PERMISSION OF THE PUBLISHER.** **To order:** Contact your local Christian bookstore; call UMI at **1-800-860-8642**; or visit our Web site at www.urbanministries.com.

TABLE OF CONTENTS

PRECEPTS FOR LIVING® PERSONAL STUDY GUIDE

TABLE OF CONTENTS

PRECEPTS FOR LIVING® PERSONAL STUDY GUIDE

INTRODUCTION

Welcome to the *Precepts For Living*® Personal Study Guide! While using it, we hope that you will find it to be an enlightening and rewarding experience. This study guide can be used as a reference tool for any teacher or student who is serious about learning and knowing the inspired Word of God. It is designed to be used in conjunction with the *Precepts For Living*® Annual Commentary. It should help you get the God-intended meaning of each Scripture presented and explained in Precepts. Therefore, it is suggested that you use the guide in the following way:

- Thoroughly study each lesson in the *Precepts For Living*® Annual Commentary. Go to the companion lesson in this study guide and answer all the questions pertaining to the lesson.

- After you have answered all the questions for a particular lesson on your own, check your answers by using the answer key, which is found in the back of this book.

- If you miss an answer, go back and research it in the *Precepts For Living*® Annual Commentary.

    This will enhance both your learning experience and memorization of Scripture.

Enjoy this *Precepts For Living*® Personal Study Guide. As you do your Bible study, observe Scripture, grasp it by correctly interpreting the text, and then walk in the knowledge of God's Word.

A VISION OF THE FUTURE

JEREMIAH 30:1–3, 18–22

Use with Bible Study Guide 1

WORDS, PHRASES, AND DEFINITIONS

Write the definition of the following words as they relate to the lesson.

1. Heap _____

2. Engaged _____

3. Captivity _____

4. Nobles _____

5. Governor _____

6. Jacob's tents _____

7. Jeremiah _____

8. Judah _____

9. Aforetime _____

10. Congregation _____

JUMP-STARTING THE LESSON

11. In the In Focus Story, Shirley is suffering but realizes she is not _____ .

12. Although Israel and Judah had been _____ for their sins, God had every intention of
_____ and _____ them. (In Focus)

UNDERSTANDING THE LESSON

13. Israel and Judah will be with His _____ and He will be their_____. (Focal Verses)

14. How many kings ruled Judah before the Babylonian captivity? (The People, Places, and Times)

    a. 30   d. 8

    b. 17   e. 20

    c. 19

15. When was Jerusalem destroyed by the Babylonian army? (The People, Places, and Times)

    a. 300 B.C.   d. A.D. 200

    b. 487 B.C.   e. 587 B.C.

    c. 676 B.C.

16. Israel's central place of worship, _____, had fallen to the _____ as punishment for the wickedness of Israel. (Background)

17. God will once again rebuild _____ , and He will do it on the "heap" or ruins of their _____ capital. (In Depth)

18. Later while in captivity in Babylonia, _____ would read Jeremiah's prophecy with a _____ heart. (More Light on the Text)

COMMITTING TO THE WORD

19. Memorize and write verbatim Jeremiah 30:22. _____

_____

_____

WALKING IN THE WORD

20. Reflect on the hope God gives in the face of an uncertain future. What does this mean in your daily life? _____

_____

_____

_____

> "Behold the days come, saith the LORD, that I will make a new covenant with the house of Israel and with the house of Judah" (Jeremiah 31:31).

RESTORATION

JEREMIAH 31:31–37

Use with Bible Study Guide 2

WORDS, PHRASES, DEFINITIONS

Write the definition of the following words as they relate to the lesson.

1. Covenant _____

2. Heart _____

3. Hosts _____

4. Babylonian Captivity _____

5. Anathoth _____

6. "I took them by the hand" _____

7. Ordinances _____

8. Divideth _____

9. Seed _____

10. Brake _____

JUMP-STARTING THE LESSON

11. At the end of the In Focus Story, Bill was happy and thankful. What did Bill thank God for?

_____

12. Though Israel had _____ sinned against Him, God wanted to _____ His covenant with them. (In Focus)

UNDERSTANDING THE LESSON

13. God will _____ the sins of His people and not _____ their wickedness. (Focal Verses)

14. The Babylonians probably only took the people who would be _____

    to them in Babylon. (The People, Places, and Times)

15. Who can make a covenant agreement? (The People, Places, and Times)

    a. Groups and nations

    b. Individuals

    c. Both of the above

16. Jeremiah was from which city? (Background)

    a. Jerusalem

    b. Babylon

    c. Bethlehem

    d. Nazareth

    e. Anathoth

17. According to the Scripture, God's people would not need to teach their _____

    because they all would _____ Him. (In Depth)

18. God's new covenant would be written on His people's _____ instead of on

    _____ like the old covenant. (More Light on the Text)

COMMITTING TO THE WORD

19. Memorize and write verbatim Jeremiah 31:33. _____

    _____

    _____

WALKING IN THE WORD

20. God gives us wonderful blessings in the new covenant. What is your favorite and why? _____

    _____

    _____

    _____

"For thus saith the LORD of hosts, the God of Israel; Houses and fields and vineyards shall be possessed again in this land" (Jeremiah 32:15).

A NEW FUTURE

JEREMIAH 32:2–9, 14–15

Use with Bible Study Guide 3

WORDS, PHRASES, DEFINITIONS

Write the definition of the following words as they relate to the lesson.

1. Besieged _____

2. Redemption _____

3. Zedekiah _____

4. Babylonia _____

5. Prophet _____

6. Nebuchadnezzar _____

7. Hanameel _____

8. Law of redemption _____

9. Visit _____

10. Shekel of silver _____

JUMP-STARTING THE LESSON

11. In the In Focus story, how did Rico display his hope in God even though the economy and housing market were in decline? _____

12. Even in _____ circumstances we can take _____ actions. (In Focus)

UNDERSTANDING THE LESSON

13. God gave His people _____ through Jeremiah's _____ action. (Focal Verses)

14. Zedekiah's real name is Mattanyahu. (The People, Places, and Times)

      TRUE   FALSE

15. The Babylonian empire finally fell to Alexander the Great. (The People, Places, and Times)

      TRUE   FALSE

16. Biblical _____ were concerned with things of the _____, _____, and _____. (Background)

17. God told Jeremiah about a _____ that his cousin would present to him concerning a portion of _____ in his hometown. (In Depth)

18. The land purchase agreement between Jeremiah and _____, witnessed by those present, would have been written down on _____ documents. (More Light on the Text)

COMMITTING TO THE WORD

Fill in the blanks.

19. "For thus saith the LORD of_____, the God of Israel; _____ and fields and _____ shall be _____ again in this land" (Jeremiah 32:15, KJV).

WALKING IN THE WORD

20. Hope can be seen in our actions. What hopeful actions can you take today concerning a situation you may be facing? _____

_____

_____

_____

"Call unto me, and I will answer thee, and show thee great and mighty things, which thou knowest not" (Jeremiah 33:3).

IMPROBABLE PROBABILITIES

JEREMIAH 33:2–11

Use with Bible Study Guide 4

WORDS, PHRASES, DEFINITIONS

Write the definition of the following words as they relate to the lesson.

1. Iniquity _____

2. Prosperity _____

3. Reveal _____

4. Chaldea _____

5. LORD _____

6. Knowest _____

7. Mounts _____

8. Peace _____

9. Truth _____

10. Pardon _____

JUMP-STARTING THE LESSON

11. In the In Focus Story, what did Carolyn ask God to do for her? _____
_____

12. God is _____ to forgive and bring recovery, healing, and _____. (In Focus)

UNDERSTANDING THE LESSON

13. God promised to _____ and _____ Judah. (Focal Verses)

14. The Northern Kingdom and Southern Kingdom separated after the reign of what king? (The People, Places, and Times)

    a. Saul   d. Zedekiah

    b. Josiah   e. Solomon

    c. Ahab

15. Mesopotamia did NOT include which of the following modern nations? (The People, Places, and Times)

    a. Iraq

    b. Syria

    c. Iran

    d. Turkey

    e. Pakistan

16. Whenever the Bible uses the name _____, there's a prevailing _____ for God's people. (Background)

17. God seeks and is able to _____ His children to their _____ place even when we fall short. (In Depth)

18. God will return the _____ of the land and restore them to a condition that will equal their state when they first _____ the Promised Land. (More Light on the Text)

COMMITTING TO THE WORD

19. Memorize and write verbatim Jeremiah 33:6. _____

_____

_____

WALKING WITH THE WORD

20. Reflect on how God forgave, restored, and healed Israel. In what places do you need God's forgiveness, restoration, and healing? _____

_____

_____

"Although the fig tree shall not blossom, neither shall fruit be in the vines … Yet I will rejoice in the LORD, I will joy in the God of my salvation" (from Habakkuk 3:17–18).

REJOICE ANYWAY

HABAKKUK 2:1–5, 3:17–19

Use with Bible Study Guide 5

WORDS, PHRASES, DEFINITIONS

Write the definition of the following words as they relate to the lesson.

1. Vision _____

2. Faith _____

3. Habakkuk _____

4. Reproved _____

5. Tables _____

6. Hind _____

7. Stringed instruments _____

8. Proud _____

9. Tower _____

10. Tarry/Be delayed _____

JUMP-STARTING THE LESSON

11. Michael began to shout "Hallelujah!" and "Thank You, Jesus!" as an act of _____ in God's _____. (In Focus)

12. Praise God for what He has _____. Praise God for what He is _____. Praise God for what He will _____ (In Focus)

UNDERSTANDING THE LESSON

13. Habakkuk will _____ in God even in times of _____. (Focal Verses)

14. Habakkuk's name means "embrace" or "ardent embrace." (The People, Places, and Times)

       TRUE   FALSE

15. The wickedness of Judah came after a period of brief reform by which king of Judah? (Background)

    a. Solomon

    b. Jehosophat

    c. Nebuchadnezzar

    d. Darius

    e. Josiah

16. Habakkuk is given _____ that the vision will come to pass in God's _____. (In Depth)

17. Trust will _____ the _____ from the _____. (In Depth)

18. The Hebrew word for faith encompasses both _____ and _____. (More Light on the Text)

COMMITTING TO THE WORD

19. Memorize and write verbatim Habakkuk 2:4. _____

_____

_____

_____

WALKING IN THE WORD

20. How can you find your joy in God during hard times? _____

_____

_____

"For I know that my redeemer liveth, and that he shall stand at the latter day upon the earth" (Job 19:25).

Even So My Redeemer Lives

JOB 19:1–7, 23–29

Use with Bible Study Guide 6

WORDS, PHRASES, DEFINITIONS

Write the definition of the following words as they relate to the lesson.

1. Reproach _____

2. Latter Day _____

3. Redeemer _____

4. Job _____

5. Break _____

6. Erred _____

7. Overthrown _____

8. Reins _____

JUMP-STARTING THE LESSON

9. In the In Focus story, Angela was singing in the car while driving home. What gave her hope?

_____

10. Even in suffering, God gives us _____ and the ability to look toward

_____. (In Focus)

UNDERSTANDING THE LESSON

11. Job believed he would see God while in his _____. (Focal Verses)

12. What was the name of the land Job lived in? (The People, Places, and Times)
   a. Assyria

b. Egypt

c. Gilead

d. Ur

e. Uz

13. David is often spoken of as a kinsman-redeemer. (The People, Places, and Times)

      TRUE   FALSE

14. Job had experienced the destruction of his wealth, his _____, and his _____. (Background)

15. Job says God is like a _____ who trapped him in his net. (In Depth)

16. Job uses the term _____ in reference to God. (In Depth)

17. When Job says his friends have accused him _____ times it is not an exact number but a Hebrew _____. (More Light on the Text)

18. Only God could _____ Job of his _____. (More Light on the Text)

COMMITTING TO THE WORD

19. Memorize and write verbatim Job 19:26. _____

_____

_____

WALKING IN THE WORD

20. Reflect on God being our kinsman-redeemer. What does this mean in your daily life? _____

_____

_____

_____

"Why, seeing times are not hidden from the Almighty, do they that know him not see his days?" (Job 24:1).

HOPE COMPLAINS

JOB 24:1, 9–12, 19–25

Use with Bible Study Guide 7

WORDS, PHRASES, DEFINITIONS

Write the definition of the following words as they relate to the lesson.

1. Almighty _____

2. Grave _____

3. Drought _____

4. Pledge _____

5. Uz _____

6. Sheaf _____

7. Winepress _____

8. Entreateth evil _____

9. Drought _____

10. Pluck _____

JUMP-STARTING THE LESSON

11. In the In Focus story, how did Pastor Johnson help Craig reintegrate into society? _____
_____

12. Job analyzed the _____ and demanded that God bring _____
to the oppressed. (In Focus)

UNDERSTANDING THE LESSON

13. Job complained of pervasive _____. (Focal Verses)

14. What could not be taken as pledge? (The People, Places, and Times)

    a. A staff

    b. A camel

    c. A widow's clothing

    d. A loaf of bread

    e. A hat

15. Uz is sometimes thought of as part of Edom (The People, Places, and Times)

          TRUE   FALSE

16. Job's friends _____, Bildad, and Zophar mourned with him over his great loss. (Background)

17. Injustice has been committed and Job looks to the _____ power and authority in the universe to right the _____ on the earth. (In Depth)

18. The entire book of Job wrestles with the problem of _____. (More Light on the Text)

COMMITTING TO THE WORD

19. Memorize and write verbatim Job 24:25. _____

_____

_____

WALKING IN THE WORD

20. Job complained to God about the injustice around Him. How do you maintain your hope in God with injustice all around you? _____

_____

_____

_____

> "And the LORD turned the captivity of Job, when he prayed for his friends: also the LORD gave Job twice as much as he had before" (Job 42:10).

HOPE SATISFIES

JOB 42:1–10

Use with Bible Study Guide 8

WORDS, PHRASES, DEFINITIONS

Write the definition of the following words as they relate to the lesson.

1. Abhor _____

2. Burnt offering _____

3. Dust and ashes _____

4. Eliphaz, Bildad, and Zophar _____

5. Repent _____

6. Seven bulls and seven rams _____

7. Hideth _____

8. Jemima _____

9. Kezia _____

10. Karen-happuch _____

JUMP-STARTING THE LESSON

11. How was Deborah's hope in the Lord's goodness rewarded? _____ (In Focus)

12. Job's hope in the Lord was _____ . (In Focus)

UNDERSTANDING THE LESSON

13. The Lord gave Job _____ what he had before. (Focal Verses)

14. Dust and ashes were worn during times of celebration. (The People, Places, and Times)
    TRUE   FALSE

15. Eliphaz, Bildad, and Zophar mourned with Job for how many days? (The People, Places, and Times)

  a. Six

  b. Four

  c. Two

  d. Seven

  e. Five

16. God asked Job a series of _____ that no _____ could possibly answer. (Background)

17. The Lord calls Job's _____ to account for their bad _____ and counsel (In Depth)

18. To see our _____ God for who He really is always causes us to realize how _____ we are in comparison. (More Light on the Text)

COMMITTING TO THE WORD

19. Memorize and write verbatim Job 42:5. _____

_____

_____

WALKING IN THE WORD

20. Job suffered immensely and was rewarded. Write about a time in your life when your hope was rewarded.

_____

_____

_____

_____

"So the spirit took me up, and brought me into the inner court; and, behold, the glory of the LORD filled the house" (Ezekiel 43:5).

GOD'S DIVINE GLORY RETURNS

EZEKIEL 43:1–12

Use With Bible Study Guide 9

WORDS, PHRASES, DEFINITIONS

Write the definition of the following words as they relate to the lesson.

1. Glory _____

2. Abominations _____

3. Inner court _____

4. Chebar river _____

5. East _____

6. Parousia _____

7. Dwell _____

8. Whoredom _____

9. Defiled _____

10. Threshold _____

JUMP-STARTING THE LESSON

11. What reminded Roger of the days when he passionately followed Jesus? _____
_____ (In Focus)

12. Although God is _____, certain places remind us of His _____ and encourage us to live holy lives before Him. (In Focus)

UNDERSTANDING THE LESSON

13. The Lord said He would _____ in the temple. (Focal Verses)

14. The inner court contained _____. (The People, Places, and Times)
    a. Sacred robes
    b. Golden staff
    c. A golden lampstand
    d. A purple rug
    e. The Shekinah glory

15. The River Chebar ran through the land of the Chaldeans. (The People, Places, and Times)
    　　　　　TRUE　　　　　　　FALSE

16. The glory of God came to the _____ and as a result it was _____ of life. (Background)

17. The proper _____ to experiencing the glory of God is _____ worship. (In Depth)

18. The whole purpose of the restored _____ would be to _____ God's glory. (More Light on the Text)

COMMITTING TO THE WORD

19. Memorize and write verbatim Ezekiel 43:2. _____
    _____
    _____
    _____

WALKING IN THE WORD

20. Reflect on the truth that God uses different places to remind us of His presence. What does this mean in your daily life? _____
    _____
    _____
    _____

"And when these days were expired, it shall be, that upon the eighth day, and so forward, the priests shall make your burnt offerings upon the altar, and your peace offerings; and I will accept you, saith the Lord GOD" (Ezekiel 43:27).

THE ALTAR, A SIGN OF HOPE

EZEKIEL 43:13–21

Use with Bible Study Guide 10

WORDS, PHRASES, DEFINITIONS

Write the definition of the following words as they relate to the lesson.

1. Horns _____

2. Bullock _____

3. Altar _____

4. Sin offering _____

5. Cubit _____

6. Bottom _____

7. Settle _____

8. Zadok _____

9. Handbreadth _____

10. Purge _____

JUMP-STARTING THE LESSON

11. In the In Focus Story, what was Rashaunda longing to experience? _____

_____

12. We often need to find _____ space for reflecting on and _____

our relationship with God. (In Focus)

UNDERSTANDING THE LESSON

13. God gives _____ for the altar. (Focal Verses)

14. Altars were made of which type of material? (The People, Places, and Times)

    a. Hewn stone

    b. Earth

    c. Metal

    d. Unhewn stone

    e. All of the above

15. What animal was used for a sin offering? (The People, Places, and Times)

    a. Gazelle

    b. Horse

    c. Donkey

    d. Bullock

    e. Two sparrows

16. Ezekiel was approached by a _____ messenger who took him toward the

    _____ Gate. (Background)

17. Ezekiel communicates the _____ measurements of the altar. (In Depth)

18. The priests, as well as the altar, were to be _____ and _____.

    (More Light on the Text)

COMMITTING TO THE WORD

19. Memorize and write verbatim Ezekiel 43:18. _____

    _____

    _____

    _____

WALKING IN THE WORD

20. We all need a personal space to reflect on and renew our relationship with God. What does this

    mean for your daily life? _____

    _____

    _____

> *"And it shall come to pass, that every thing that liveth … shall live: and there shall be a very great multitude of fish, because these waters shall come thither: for they shall be healed; and every thing shall live whither the river cometh"* (Ezekiel 47:9).

A TRANSFORMING STREAM

EZEKIEL 47:1, 3–12

Use with Bible Study Guide 11

WORDS, PHRASES, DEFINITIONS

Write the definition of the following words as they relate to the lesson.

1. Ezekiel _____

2. House _____

3. Loins _____

4. En Gedi _____

5. Eneglaim _____

6. Meat _____

7. Sanctuary _____

8. Dead Sea _____

9. Miry places _____

10. Marshes _____

JUMP-STARTING THE LESSON

11. What happened to Sharla after she prayed and experienced a few moments of silence?

_____ (In Focus)

12. God is the _____ of everything we _____. (In Focus)

UNDERSTANDING THE LESSON

13. God _____ healing and _____ to His people. (Focal Verses)

14. Ezekiel was an active prophet of God in Babylon for how many years? (The People, Places, and Times)

    a. Sixty

    b. Ten

    c. Twenty-five

    d. Twenty-two

15. Ezekiel's vision of the river is the second major vision in the book. (The People, Places, and Times)

    TRUE   FALSE

16. The flow of God's Spirit through _____ brings _____ life and healing to all who will accept Him. (In Depth)

17. The _____ that proceed from God have a healing, _____ effect. (In Depth)

18. With each step of _____, Ezekiel finds himself going _____ into dependence on the grace of God. (More Light on the Text)

COMMITTING TO THE WORD

19. Memorize and write verbatim Ezekiel 47:5. _____

_____

_____

_____

WALKING IN THE WORD

20. Reflect on the healing and refreshment given by God's Spirit. How can you access this in your daily life? _____

_____

_____

_____

"So shall ye divide this land unto you ... and to the strangers that sojourn among you" (Ezekiel 47:21–22).

TRANSFORMATION CONTINUED

EZEKIEL 47:13–23

Use with Bible Study Guide 12

WORDS, PHRASES, DEFINITIONS

Write the definition of the following words as they relate to the lesson.

1. Fellowship _____

2. Inheritance _____

3. Lebo-Hamath _____

4. Kadesh Barnea _____

5. Damascus _____

6. Waters of strife _____

7. Strangers _____

8. Joseph _____

9. Divide by lot _____

10. The Great Sea _____

JUMP-STARTING THE LESSON

11. In the In Focus story, what caused Andrea's eyes to be filled with tears? _____
_____ (In Focus)

12. God wants His _____ to be a loving _____ where people can find support to make a new beginning. (In Focus)

UNDERSTANDING THE LESSON

13. God gave an _____ of land to Israel. (Focal Verses)

14. The Mediterranean Sea was the boundary for Israel in which direction? (The People, Places, and Times)

    a. East

    b. South

    c. North

    d. West

    e. All of the above

15. Who would now be included in the new inheritance? (Background)

    a. Manasseh

    b. Levites

    c. Gilead

    d. Dan

    e. Gentiles

16. The inheritance was a _____ from God, and He is _____ to do what He has promised. (In Depth)

17. In this renewed _____, any inequities would be a _____ memory. (More Light on the Text)

18. Ezekiel's vision was the _____ of a new _____. (More Light on the Text)

COMMITTING TO THE WORD

19. Memorize and write verbatim Ezekiel 47:14. _____

    _____

    _____

    _____

WALKING IN THE WORD

20. All believers have a spiritual inheritance. Write out the details of your inheritance in Christ.

    _____

    _____

    _____

> "How beautiful upon the mountains are the feet of him that bringeth good tidings, that publisheth peace; that bringeth good tidings of good, that publisheth salvation; that saith unto Zion, Thy God reigneth!" (Isaiah 52:7).

LET ZION REJOICE

ISAIAH 52:1–2, 7–12

Use with Bible Study Guide 13

WORDS, PHRASES, DEFINITIONS

Write the definition of the following words as they relate to the lesson.

1. Uncircumcised _____

2. Unclean _____

3. Watchman _____

4. Jerusalem _____

5. Zion _____

6. Beauty _____

7. Strength _____

8. "Made bare his holy arm" _____

9. Reward _____

10. "Vessels of the Lord" _____

JUMP-STARTING THE LESSON

11. In the In Focus story, what did Chauntel do after reading Hakim's letter? What caused this

    reaction? _____

12. The people of God have good cause for _____ . They have received His Good

    News of _____.

UNDERSTANDING THE LESSON

13. God _____ and _____ His people. (Focal Verses)

14. Zion is a name for what? (The People, Places, and Times)

    a. Gentiles

    b. The lost tribes of Israel

    c. Church

    d. The heavenly city

    e. Both c. and d.

15. How many times was Jerusalem destroyed? (The People, Places, and Times)

    a. Once

    b. Three times

    c. Twice

    d. Five times

    e. Never

16. The Babylonian _____ was brought to a close after the fall of Babylon to _____ the Great. (Background)

17. After _____ years of captivity, Isaiah states, the _____ or ruined places of Jerusalem will begin to sing. (In Depth)

18. As sovereign, God is the one who _____ the future. (More Light on the Text)

COMMITTING TO THE WORD

19. Memorize and write verbatim Isaiah 52:12. _____

_____

_____

WALKING IN THE WORD

21. The Israelites rejoiced at the good news. What gives you cause for rejoicing? _____

_____

_____

_____

> *"[Jesus] being the brightness of his glory, and the express image of his person, and upholding all things with the word of his power, when he had by himself purged our sins, sat down on the right hand of the Majesty on high" (Hebrews 1:3).*

WORSHIP CHRIST'S MAJESTY

HEBREWS 1:1–9

Use with Bible Study Guide 1

WORDS, PHRASES, DEFINITIONS

Write the definition of the following words as they relate to the lesson.

1. Majesty _____

2. Angel _____

3. Sin _____

4. Purification rituals _____

5. "In these last days" _____

6. Worlds _____

7. "Express image of his person" _____

8. "Majesty on high" _____

9. Purged _____

10. Ministers _____

JUMP-STARTING THE LESSON

11. What title did President Clinton award to Maya Angelou? (In Focus) _____

12. Why is Jesus worthy of our highest honor and worship? (In Focus) _____

_____

UNDERSTANDING THE LESSON

13. God has given _____ a name greater than the _____. (Focal Verses)

14. What was the primary duty of the priests of Israel? (The People, Places, and Times)

    a. Teach the people

    b. Wear God-honoring clothing

    c. Collect tithes

    d. Sacrifice an animal for the forgiveness of sins

    e. Discover the will of God

15. What replaces the purification rituals as a means to access a holy God? (The People, Places, and Times)

    a. Church attendance

    b. Communion

    c. Sacrificial giving

    d. Jesus' sacrifice

    e. Baptism

16. Jesus' _____ are connected to the very _____ of God. (In Depth)

17. Jesus is _____ to angels because His _____ is connected directly and inseparably to God. (In Depth)

18. Jesus is not only _____ of the universe, but He is also _____ it by His Word. (More Light on the Text)

COMMITTING TO THE WORD

19. Memorize and write verbatim Hebrews 1:1–2. _____

_____

_____

WALKING IN THE WORD

20. Reflect on the truth that Jesus is worthy of our highest honor and worship. How can you honor Him in your daily life? _____

_____

_____

"O come, let us sing to the LORD: let us make a joyful noise to the rock of our salvation" (Psalm 95:1).

MAKE A JOYFUL NOISE

PSALM 95:1–7a

Use with Bible Study Guide 2

WORDS, PHRASES, DEFINITIONS

Write the definition of the following words as they relate to the lesson.

1. Psalms _____

2. Thanksgiving _____

3. Gods _____

4. Pasture _____

5. "Rock of our salvation" _____

6. Meribah _____

7. "Joyful noise" _____

8. Worship _____

9. "Deep places of the earth" _____

10. Kneel _____

JUMP-STARTING THE LESSON

11. What excuse did David give his pastor for resigning from the music team? (In Focus) _____

_____

12. We must _____ that we _____ God in spirit and in truth. (In Focus)

UNDERSTANDING THE LESSON

13. The Lord is a great _____ above all gods. (Focal Verses)

14. The Israelites declared their one God as supreme over the many gods of other nations. (The People, Places, and Times)

        TRUE   FALSE

15. The best pasture in Palestine was found in what location? (The People, Places, and Times)
    a. The desert near Egypt
    b. Close to the beach
    c. The mountains of Syria and Palestine
    d. The plateaus east of the Jordan
    e. Both c. and d.

16. One cannot _____ God with a hardened _____ as this psalm warns. (Background)

17. The tools that the psalmist prescribes to be used in worship are _____ and _____. (In Depth)

18. The psalmist is filled with such _____ at God's power that _____ are not enough. (More Light on the Text)

COMMITTING TO THE WORD

19. Memorize and write verbatim Psalm 95:3. _____

_____

_____

WALKING IN THE WORD

20. The presence of God provokes worship. What are some of the ways that you worship God? _____

_____

_____

_____

_____

GLORY TO GOD IN THE HIGHEST

LUKE 2:8–20

"And the shepherds returned, glorifying and praising God for all the things that they had heard and seen, as it was told unto them" (Luke 2:20).

Use with Bible Study Guide 3

WORDS, DEFINITIONS, PHRASES

Write the definition of the following words as they relate to the lesson.

1. Joy _____

2. Messiah _____

3. Shepherds _____

4. Bethlehem _____

5. Glory _____

6. "Bring good tidings" _____

7. Saviour _____

8. Lord _____

9. Good will _____

10. Kept _____

JUMP-STARTING THE LESSON

11. What was in the envelope that Gina received from her college friend? (In Focus) _____
_____

12. The coming of Jesus brings _____ news to the world. (In Focus)

UNDERSTANDING THE LESSON

13. The _____ received the news about the birth of the _____.
(Focal Verses)

14. A shepherd's job was very honorable and brought a great measure of wealth. (The People, Places, and Times)

    TRUE   FALSE

15. Historically, Bethlehem was also known by which name? (The People, Places, and Times)
    a. City of Shepherds
    b. House of Olives
    c. Place of Kings
    d. City of David

16. Pregnant Mary and Joseph had to travel at least _____ miles from Nazareth to Bethlehem. (Background)

17. The angel of the Lord quickly reassured these_____ shepherds by announcing good news of _____ joy. (In Depth)

18. Shepherds at the time of Jesus were not only _____ but were also considered _____. (More Light on the Text)

COMMITTING TO THE WORD

19. Memorize and write verbatim Luke 2:14._____
    _____
    _____

WALKING IN THE WORD

20. Reflect on the Good News of Christ's birth. How can you share the Good News with others? _____
    _____
    _____
    _____
    _____
    _____

> "And when they were come into the ship the wind ceased. Then they that were in the ship came and worshipped Him, saying, Of a truth thou art the Son of God" (Matthew 14:32–3).

IN AWE OF CHRIST'S POWER

MATTHEW 14:22–36

Use with Bible Study Guide 4

WORDS, PHRASES, DEFINITIONS

Write the definition of the following words as they relate to the lesson.

1. Gennesaret _____

2. "Of little faith" _____

3. Sea of Galilee _____

4. Hem _____

5. Constrained _____

6. Evening _____

7. Spirit _____

8. "Be of good cheer" _____

9. Worship _____

10. Diseased _____

JUMP-STARTING THE LESSON

11. In the In Focus story, what did Warren decide to do instead of being angry and frustrated with God? _____

12. The Lord has the _____ to do the _____ in our lives. (In Focus)

UNDERSTANDING THE LESSON

13. Jesus did the _____ by _____ on water. (Focal Verses)

14. The Sea of Galilee was located in what direction from Jerusalem? (The People, Places, and Times)

    a. East

    b. West

    c. North

    d. South

15. What was Peter's birth name? (The People, Places, and Times)

    a. Matthias

    b. Jonah

    c. Levi

    d. Simon

    e. Both a. and d.

16. The One who created the _____ has the power to walk on them and is _____ over all the earth. (In Depth).

17. The Lord wants us to "be of good _____" and not be afraid because of His _____. (More Light on the Text)

18. We can perform _____ works by faith as long as we keep _____ at the Lord who instructs us. (More Light on the Text)

COMMITTING TO THE WORD

19. Memorize and write verbatim Matthew 14:31._____

    _____

    _____

WALKING IN THE WORD

20. Reflect on the truth that Jesus can do the impossible. How can you apply this truth to your life?

    _____

    _____

    _____

    _____

A MODEL FOR PRAYER

LUKE 11:1–13

"And he said unto them, When ye pray, say, Our Father who art in heaven, Hallowed be your name, Thy kingdom come. Thy will be done, as in heaven, so in earth" (Luke 11:2).

Use with Bible Study Guide 5

WORDS, DEFINITIONS, PHRASES

Write the definition of the following words as they relate to the lesson.

1. "Our Father" _____

2. "Hallowed be" _____

3. Heaven _____

4. Disciples _____

5. Kingdom of God _____

6. Daily _____

7. Temptation _____

8. Forgive _____

9. Importunity _____

10. Knock _____

JUMP-STARTING THE LESSON

11. In the In Focus Story, what caused Imani to recognize her mother's faith in God? _____

_____

12. Our _____ with God is _____ through prayer. (In Focus)

UNDERSTANDING THE LESSON

13. Everyone who _____ receives an _____ to prayer. (Focal Verses)

14. What's another word for disciple? (The People, Places, and Times)

    a. Promoter

    b. Apostle

    c. Church member

    d. Fan

    e. Follower

15. How many times is the phrase "Kingdom of God" mentioned in Mark and Luke's Gospels? (The People, Places, and Times)

    a. 20

    b. 100

    c. 57

    d. 46

    e. 10

16. _____ is a major theme of Luke's Gospel. (Background)

17. To _____ God for something is to come to Him knowing that He is able to _____. (In Depth)

18. The _____ Jesus' prayer life _____ has motivated a disciple for a teaching on the subject. (More Light On The Text)

COMMITTING TO THE WORD

19. Memorize and write verbatim Luke 11:10. _____

_____

_____

WALKING IN THE WORD

20. God asks us to pray for our daily bread. Write out how God has provided for your need. _____

_____

_____

_____

JESUS PRAYS FOR HIS DISCIPLES

JOHN 17:6–21

"That they may all be one; as thou, Father, art in me, and I in thee, that they also may be one in us; that the world may believe that thou hast sent me" (John 17:21).

Use with Bible Study Guide 6

WORDS, PHRASES, DEFINITIONS

Write the definition of the following words as they relate to the lesson.

1. Pray _____

2. Glorify _____

3. John _____

4. Name _____

5. Manifested _____

6. Sanctify _____

7. Sent _____

8. One _____

9. "Evil one" _____

10. "Son of perdition" _____

JUMP-STARTING THE LESSON

11. How does Ashley benefit from having Morgan pray for her on a weekly basis? (In Focus) _____
_____

12. Jesus prayed not only for His _____ but for those who would _____
based on their witness. (In Focus)

UNDERSTANDING THE LESSON

13. Jesus prays for the _____ of all believers. (Focal Verses)

14. John was exiled to which island? (The People, Places, and Times)

    a. Crete

    b. Cyprus

    c. Malta

    d. Rhodes

    e. Patmos

15. Jesus is portrayed as one who stays in complete _____ with the Father and is singularly focused on _____ the Father's will. (Background)

16. The unity of the believers would _____ whether Jesus was sent from God and would cause the world to _____ on Him as Savior. (In Depth)

17. Jesus prays that we as believers would be _____ and close just as the first and second Persons of the _____. (In Depth)

18. Jesus prayed for the _____ of the disciples from _____ and the evil one. (More Light on the Text)

COMMITTING TO THE WORD

19. Memorize and write verbatim John 17:9. _____

_____

_____

WALKING IN THE WORD

20. Jesus prayed that all believers would be one. How can you show your unity with other believers who are different from you?_____

_____

_____

_____

> *"For we have not an high priest which cannot be touched with the feeling of our infirmities; but was in all points tempted like we are, yet without sin" (Hebrews 4:15).*

JESUS INTERCEDES FOR US

HEBREWS 4:14–5:10

Use with Bible Study Guide 7

WORDS, PHRASES, DEFINITIONS

Write the definition of the following words as they relate to the lesson.

1. High priest _____

2. Order _____

3. Melchizedek _____

4. Compassion _____

5. Called _____

6. "In the days of his flesh" _____

7. Feared _____

8. "Being made perfect" _____

9. "Eternal salvation" _____

10. Author _____

JUMP-STARTING THE LESSON

11. In the In Focus story, what caused Aiesha to not cave in to peer pressure? _____ (In Focus)

12. Jesus is both our _____ brother and _____. (In Focus)

UNDERSTANDING THE LESSON

13. Jesus is our _____ High Priest. (Focal Verses)

14. What did Melchizedek offer to Abraham? (The People, Places, and Times)

    a. Fish

    b. Honey

    c. Lamb

    d. Bread and wine

    e. None of the above

15. The book of Hebrews was tailored and penned to _____ a primarily _____ audience. (Background)

16. Jesus in His _____ as our High Priest puts an end to the need to _____ anyone else for the forgiveness of sins. (In Depth)

17. The high priest _____ a year entered the Holy of Holies to make _____ of sins for himself and the sins of the people. (In Depth)

18. Unlike Aaron, _____ was both _____ and priest. (More Light on the Text)

COMMITTING TO THE WORD

19. Memorize and write verbatim Hebrews 4:16. _____

_____

_____

_____

WALKING IN THE WORD

20. Jesus is our High Priest making intercession for us. What are the benefits of having Jesus as our great High Priest? _____

_____

_____

_____

_____

WE PRAY FOR ONE ANOTHER

JAMES 5:13–18

> *"Confess your faults to one another, and pray for one another, that ye may be healed. The effectual fervent prayer of a righteous man availeth much" (James 5:16).*

Use with Bible Study Guide 8

WORDS, PHRASES, DEFINITIONS

Write the definition of the following words as they relate to the lesson.

1. Sick _____

2. Fervent _____

3. Elders _____

4. Anointing _____

5. Elias _____

6. Afflicted _____

7. Oil _____

8. "Shall raise him up" _____

9. Confess _____

10. Faults _____

JUMP-STARTING THE LESSON

11. In the In Focus story, what were the reasons Latonya had for not praying for healing? _____
_____ (In Focus)

12. If we have a _____ with God, then His _____
to heal is available for all those who believe. (In Focus)

UNDERSTANDING THE LESSON

13. God _____ effectual fervent prayer. (Focal Verses)

14. In the New Testament, the terms bishops, elders, and presbyters are used interchangeably. (The People, Places, and Times)

  TRUE FALSE

15. James has been called the _____ of the New Testament because it is full of _____ and practical teaching about the Christian life. (Background)

16. Effective prayers are those that _____ up with God's will and _____ results. (In Depth)

17. The Christian should _____ God to heal and _____ sin. (In Depth)

18. Before prayer changes the _____, prayer changes the _____. (More Light on the Text)

COMMITTING TO THE WORD

19. Memorize and write verbatim James 5:15. _____

_____

_____

WALKING IN THE WORD

20. James says the effectual fervent prayer of the righteous produces results. How can you make sure your prayers are effectual and fervent? _____

_____

_____

_____

_____

"But thou, when thou fastest, anoint thine head, and wash thy face; That thou appear not unto men to fast, but unto thy Father which is in secret: and thy Father, which seeth in secret, shall reward thee openly" (Matthew 6:17–18).

FEASTING AND FASTING

Daniel 1:5, 8–17; Matthew 6:16–18

Use with Bible Study Guide 9

WORDS, PHRASES, DEFINITIONS

Write the definition of the following words as it relates to the lesson:

1. Pulse _____

2. Eunuch _____

3. Nebuchadnezzar _____

4. Defile _____

5. Melzar _____

6. Fasting _____

7. Hananiah, Mishael, and Azariah _____

8. Hypocrite _____

9. Kosher _____

10. Yom Kippur _____

JUMP-STARTING THE LESSON

11. In the In Focus Story, Debroah learned fasting was about _____ herself to have a

    closer _____ with God.

12. Rather than just abstaining from certain foods, fasting is _____ . (In Focus)

UNDERSTANDING THE LESSON

13. God blessed _____ when they fasted, and God will _____ when

    you fast in secret too. (Focal Verses)

14. Daniel and his friends' diet of "pulse" included what foods? (The People, Places, and Times)

    a. Vegetables

    b. Fruit

    c. Legumes

    d. Bread

    e. All of the above

15. Eunuchs were rare in royal courts of Daniel's day. (The People, Places, and Times)

         TRUE   FALSE

16. Daniel and his friends promoted the _____ God as the God of all the _____.
(Background)

17. For Daniel and his friends, though risky, it was worth it to remain _____ to God and
promote His _____ in a foreign land. (In Depth)

18. Consuming the king's portions was problematic because the meat would not be _____.
(More Light on the Text)

COMMITTING TO THE WORD

19. Memorize and write verbatim Daniel 1:17. _____

_____

_____

_____

WALKING IN THE WORD

20. In Daniel, we saw a fast helped young Hebrew captives remain loyal to God. What benefits might
fasting hold for you? _____

_____

_____

_____

> "Which now of these three, thinkest thou, was neighbour unto him that fell among the thieves? And he said, He that shewed mercy on him. Then said Jesus unto him, Go, and do thou likewise" (Luke 10:36–37).

SERVING NEIGHBORS, SERVING GOD

Luke 10:25–34

Use with Bible Study Guide 10

WORDS, PHRASES, DEFINITIONS
Define each of the following words as it relates to the lesson:

1. Lawyers _____

2. Samaritans _____

3. Compassion _____

4. Levite _____

5. Neighbor _____

6. Heart, Soul, Strength, Mind _____

7. Priest _____

8. The Shema _____

9. Tested _____

10. Ubuntu _____

JUMP-STARTING THE LESSON

11. What small act of kindness did Mary show Mr. Martinez? _____ (In Focus)

12. Christians are commanded to love both God and _____ . (In Focus)

UNDERSTANDING THE LESSON

13. A _____ and a _____ passed the injured man by before the _____ stopped and cared for him. (Focal Verses)

14. Lawyers often questioned Jesus on _____ matters. (The People, Places, and Times)

15. Samaritans mixed Jewish traditions and pagan worship habits. (The People, Places, and Times)

       TRUE   FALSE

16. The teachers of the Law, scribes, and Pharisees asked Jesus tricky questions in order to

      _____. (Background)

17. Rabbis would often answer a question with a _____ . (In Depth)

    a. Parable

    b. Question

    c. Simple answer

    d. Discussion of possibilities

18. Deuteronomy 6 contains the _____, which the lawyer cited as the first commandment.

    (More Light on the Text)

COMMITTING TO THE WORD

19. Memorize and write verbatim Luke 10:27._____

_____

_____

_____

WALKING IN THE WORD

20. Though the phrase "good Samaritan" is common for us today, it would have been quite startling

    in Jesus' day. What would you do if a person you wouldn't usually trust offered you help when you

    needed it most? _____

_____

_____

_____

"And the King shall answer and say unto them, Verily I say unto you, Inasmuch as ye have done it unto one of the least of these my brethren, ye have done it unto me" (Matthew 25:40).

SERVING THE LEAST

Matthew 25:31–46

Use with Bible Study Guide 11

WORDS, PHRASES, DEFINITIONS
Define each of the following words as it relates to the lesson:

1. Son of Man _____

2. Mount of Olives _____

3. Cursed _____

4. Inherit _____

5. Separate _____

6. Everlasting fire _____

7. Olivet Discourse _____

8. Sheep _____

9. Goats _____

10. Parabolic _____

JUMP-STARTING THE LESSON

11. To whom was James ministering? _____ (In Focus)

12. We are called to serve the least of these as if they were _____ . (In Focus)

UNDERSTANDING THE LESSON

13. As a shepherd divides the _____ from the _____, the King will

divide the _____ and the _____. (Focal Verses)

14. The phrase "Son of Man" portrays Jesus'... (The People, Places, and Times)

    a. Divinity

    b. Humanity

    c. Judaism

    d. Gentleness

15. The Mount of Olives is on the southern side of Jerusalem. (The People, Places, and Times)
    TRUE   FALSE

16. To whom does "brethren" in verse 40 refer? (Background)

    a. Only Jews

    b. Only Christians

    c. Only the Twelve

    d. It is unclear.

17. Jews are commanded to _____ for those less fortunate. (In Depth)

18. Our service to our fellow man is not just leftover _____ for those who are

    destitute but an act of service to _____. (More Light on the Text)

COMMITTING TO THE WORD

19. Memorize and write verbatim Matthew 25:34. _____

    _____

    _____

    _____

WALKING IN THE WORD

20. Do you find yourself trying to separate the "sheep" and the "goats" yourself? What criteria do you

    use? Is it the same as what God, the true Judge, uses? _____

    _____

    _____

    _____

> *"Put on the whole armour of God, that ye may be able to stand against the wiles of the devil"* (Ephesians 6:11).

CLOTHED AND READY

Ephesians 6:10–20

Use with Bible Study Guide 12

WORDS, PHRASES, DEFINITIONS

Define each of the following words as it relates to the lesson:

1. Principalities _____

2. Armor _____

3. Breastplate _____

4. Supplication _____

5. Righteousness _____

6. Shield _____

7. Mystery of the Gospel _____

8. Epistle _____

9. Spiritual warfare _____

10. Satan _____

JUMP-STARTING THE LESSON

11. Why did Dave single Clarence out? _____ (In Focus)

12. God _____ us with everything we need for the battles of life. (In Focus)

UNDERSTANDING THE LESSON

13. Paul mentions several pieces of the armor of God, including _____. (Focal Verses)

    a. The helmet of salvation and the sword of faith

    b. The sword of the Spirit and the breastplate of righteousness

    c. The shield of courage and the boots of peace

14. The principalities and powers were created by God and appear to be _____ that have rebelled against Him. (The People, Places, and Times)

15. The Roman soldier's usual spear is absent from Paul's description of the armor of God. (The People, Places, and Times)

        TRUE   FALSE

16. Paul concludes his letter with an exhortation to _____, describing the church in a _____ perspective. (Background)

17. We are called not only to look after _____ but to stand with all of our _____ in Christ. (In Depth)

18. The fiery darts of the enemy include each of the following except what? (More Light on the Text)
    a. Temptations
    b. Affection
    c. Doubt
    d. False guilt

COMMITTING TO THE WORD

19. Memorize and write verbatim Ephesians 6:12. _____
    _____
    _____
    _____

WALKING IN THE WORD

20. When we are armed with truth, righteousness, peace, salvation, faith, and the Spirit, there is no satanic attack we cannot face and defeat. Recall a time you encountered spiritual warfare in your life. _____
    _____
    _____
    _____

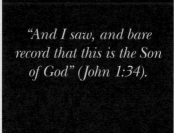

"And I saw, and bare record that this is the Son of God" (John 1:34).

THE LAMB OF GOD

John 1:29–34

Use with Bible Study Guide 1

WORDS, PHRASES, DEFINITIONS
Define each of the following words as it relates to the lesson:

1. Perea _____

2. Baptism _____

3. Jordan River _____

4. Dove _____

5. Taketh away _____

6. John the Baptist _____

7. Zacharias and Elisabeth _____

8. Lamb of God _____

9. Passover _____

10. Manifest _____

JUMP-STARTING THE LESSON

11. How did Trey's baptism affect his walk with Christ? _____ (In Focus)

12. John the Baptist announced Jesus' ministry of _____ baptism. (In Focus)

UNDERSTANDING THE LESSON

13. When John saw Jesus coming to be baptized, John said, "Behold, the Lion of God, who conquers the sins of the world." (Focal Verses)

        TRUE   FALSE

14. John baptized in an area called _____, which was a large region located east of the _____ River and to the northeast of _____. (The People, Places, and Times)

15. The act of baptism was a common _____ cleansing ritual. (The People, Places, and Times)
    a. Gentile
    b. Egyptian
    c. Celtic
    d. Jewish

16. John the Baptist lived in the wilderness, wore _____ hair, and ate _____. (Background)

17. Jesus and John the Baptist were _____ . (In Depth)
    a. Rivals
    b. Brothers
    c. Cousins
    d. Priests

18. The Holy Spirit descending and resting on Him was the sign by which John was told he would know the identity of the Christ. (More Light on the Text)
              TRUE   FALSE

COMMITTING TO THE WORD

19. Memorize and write verbatim John 1:30. _____
_____
_____
_____

WALKING IN THE WORD

20. John knew that God had called him to preach repentance and baptize. What has God called you to do for the kingdom? _____
_____
_____
_____

"But the Comforter, which is the Holy Ghost, whom the Father will send in my name, he shall teach you all things, and bring all things to your remembrance, whatsoever I have said unto you" (John 14:26).

JESUS PROMISES AN ADVOCATE

John 14:15–26

Use with Bible Study Guide 2

WORDS, PHRASES, DEFINITIONS

Define each of the following words as it relates to the lesson:

1. Fatherless _____

2. Comforter _____

3. Motif _____

4. Iscariot _____

5. Upper Room _____

6. Third Person of the Trinity _____

7. Commandment _____

8. Advocate _____

9. Comfortless _____

10. "The world" _____

JUMP-STARTING THE LESSON

11. What did the Holy Spirit lead James to do? _____ (In Focus)

12. The Holy Spirit _____ us to live God-honoring lives and gives _____. (In Focus)

UNDERSTANDING THE LESSON

13. How would the disciples be able to remember Jesus' words? _____ (Focal Verses)

14. Without a father, orphans had no one to _____ for them and no representation in _____. (The People, Places, and Times)

15. The Passover Festival reminds the Jewish people of when _____. (Background)
    a. God gave them the Law through Moses
    b. God spared their firstborn children from the tenth plague in Egypt
    c. They wandered in the wilderness for forty years
    d. Esther saved the Jews from slaughter

16. The announcement of Jesus' departure and the pending arrival of the Holy Spirit followed several events that _____ and _____ His disciples. (Background)

17. Obeying Jesus' commandments is a _____ result of the disciples' love for Him. (In Depth)

18. The Greek word *parakletos* is translated each of the following ways except _____ (More Light on the Text)
    a. Teacher
    b. Advocate
    c. Comforter
    d. Helper

COMMITTING TO THE WORD

19. Memorize and write verbatim John 14:15. _____
_____
_____
_____

WALKING IN THE WORD

20. How do you open yourself to hearing the Spirit's leading in your life? _____
_____
_____
_____

"Nevertheless I tell you the truth; It is expedient for you that I go away: for if I go not away, the Comforter will not come unto you; but if I depart, I will send him unto you" (John 16:7).

THE SPIRIT OF TRUTH

John 16:4b–15

Use with Bible Study Guide 3

WORDS, PHRASES, DEFINITIONS

Define each of the following words as it relates to the lesson:

1. Expedient _____

2. Reprove _____

3. Zebedee _____

4. "Prince of this world" _____

5. Judgment _____

6. Spirit of Truth _____

7. The Father _____

8. Legalism _____

9. Conscience _____

10. Ascension _____

JUMP-STARTING THE LESSON

11. After Ann's mother died, she saw God place _____ in her life to guide, love, encourage, and challenge her. (In Focus)

12. Christ encourages His _____ by promising to send a Helper. (In Focus)

UNDERSTANDING THE LESSON

13. What three things does Jesus say the Spirit will reprove the world of ? _____

(Focal Verses)

14. The blood of the Passover lamb was sprinkled on the _____ and in the _____. (The People, Places, and Times)

15. John 13–17 comprise a passage known as the Upper Room Discourse. (The People, Places, and Times)

          TRUE   FALSE

16. Where is the purpose of John's Gospel stated? _____ (Background)

17. In this passage, Jesus promises that the Holy Spirit will _____ . (In Depth)
    a. Guide unbelievers and guard believers
    b. Convict unbelievers and guide believers
    c. Convict both believers and unbelievers
    d. Guide both believers and unbelievers

18. It is _____ for the disciples for Jesus to leave, because the Comforter would come with a definite agenda of _____ the world. (More Light on the Text)

COMMITTING TO THE WORD

19. Memorize and write verbatim John 16:14. _____

_____

_____

_____

WALKING IN THE WORD

20. Consider the similarities and differences among the ways each Person of the Trinity interacts with God's people. _____

_____

_____

_____

_____

"And when he had said this, he breathed on them, and saith unto them, Receive ye the Holy Ghost" (John 20:22).

RECEIVE THE HOLY SPIRIT

John 20:19–23

Use with Bible Study Guide 4

WORDS, PHRASES, DEFINITIONS

Define each of the following words as it relates to the lesson:

1. Resurrection _____

2. "The Jews" _____

3. Pentecost _____

4. Shalom _____

5. Remit _____

6. Retain _____

7. Nicodemus _____

8. Mary Magdalene _____

9. Show _____

10. Send _____

JUMP-STARTING THE LESSON

11. How did Ama pass on the hope that Joy had given her? _____ (In Focus)

12. The Holy Spirit can empower us to make a difference, for _____ . (In Focus)

UNDERSTANDING THE LESSON

13. Jesus greeted His disciples with the words " _____ ." (Focal Verses)

   a. Rejoice, friends

   b. Hail, mighty men of valor

   c. Peace be unto you

14. Christ's resurrection was not bodily but spiritual. (The People, Places, and Times)

        TRUE   FALSE

15. The majority of the Jewish _____ were responsible for provoking the people to call for Jesus' death. (The People, Places, and Times)

16. Like many Jews, the disciples were expecting Jesus to be a triumphant _____ who would free them from the oppressive _____, and usher in a new worldly kingdom (Background)

17. Jesus' appearance and greeting to His disciples assured them that _____ . (In Depth)
    a. They did not need to fear that He was a ghost
    b. He was alive
    c. He is divine
    d. All the above.

18. By breathing on them, Jesus foreshadows what would happen some weeks later on the day of _____. (More Light on the Text)

COMMITTING TO THE WORD

19. Memorize and write verbatim John 20:21. _____
_____
_____
_____

WALKING IN THE WORD

20. Jesus empowered His followers to receive the Holy Spirit. What does having the Holy Spirit mean in your life? _____
_____
_____
_____

"And they that went before, and they that followed, cried, saying, Hosanna; Blessed is he that cometh in the name of the Lord" (Mark 11:9).

THE ONE WHO COMES

Mark 11:1–11

Use with Bible Study Guide 5

WORDS, PHRASES, DEFINITIONS

Define each of the following words as it relates to the lesson:

1. Victory processions _____

2. Palm tree _____

3. Gospel of Mark _____

4. Bethphage _____

5. Bethany _____

6. Hosanna _____

7. Feast of Tabernacles _____

8. Colt _____

9. Sabbath day's journey _____

10. Hallel _____

JUMP-STARTING THE LESSON

11. Who finally got Donna to reconsider her devotion to her favorite player? _____ (In Focus)

12. We should all live to _____ Christ as the One who came to save us. (In Focus)

UNDERSTANDING THE LESSON

13. After entering Jerusalem and coming to the temple, Jesus left the city and returned to

_____ . (Focal Verses)

14. The palm tree was an ancient symbol of victory. (The People, Places, and Times)
    TRUE   FALSE

15. Mark asserts that the Messiah's purpose was to _____, _____, and
    _____ to ensure eternal salvation. (The People, Places, and Times)

16. Jesus and His disciples journeyed to _____ for the Passover. (Background)

17. Mark primarily depicts Jesus as the _____ . (In Depth)
    a. King of creation
    b. Suffering Servant
    c. Son of Man
    d. Son of God

18. Jesus' humble Triumphal Entry was very different from the triumph parades of Roman
    _____. (More Light on the Text)

COMMITTING TO THE WORD

19. Memorize and write verbatim Mark 11:10._____
    _____
    _____
    _____

WALKING IN THE WORD

20. Jesus showed His humility by choosing to ride a donkey into Jerusalem. How can you show such
    humility in your life?_____
    _____
    _____
    _____

RESURRECTION GUARANTEED

"For as in Adam all die, even so in Christ shall all be made alive" (1 Corinthians 15:22).

1 Corinthians 15:1–11, 20–22

Use with Bible Study Guide 6

WORDS, PHRASES, DEFINITIONS

Define each of the following words as it relates to the lesson:

1. Gospel _____

2. Paul _____

3. Apostolic _____

4. Eschatological _____

5. Firstfruits _____

6. Cephas _____

7. Adam _____

8. Corinth _____

9. James _____

10. The Twelve _____

JUMP-STARTING THE LESSON

11. Melissa was excited to finally meet everyone from her _____ side of the family. (In Focus)

12. The _____ of Christ defines our Christian identity. (In Focus)

UNDERSTANDING THE LESSON

13. After His resurrection, Jesus was seen by all of the following except _____ . (Focal Verses)

    a. James

    b. 500 believers

    c. Peter

    d. Pontius Pilate

14. Another historically significant use of the word "gospel" was to announce that _____ was the new emperor of Rome. (The People, Places, and Times)

15. Prior to his conversion, Paul (then called Saul) was a Pharisee who zealously persecuted Christians. (The People, Places, and Times)

           TRUE   FALSE

16. Which of the following issues had Paul NOT discussed in 1 Corinthians before turning to the Resurrection? (Background)

    a. Giving to the Jerusalem church

    b. Incest

    c. Speaking in tongues

    d. Divisions in the church

17. In this passage, Paul explains the foundation of the Christian faith: 1) Christ _____; 2) Christ _____; 3) Christ _____. (In Depth)

18. Instead of relying on his own authority, Paul argues for the Resurrection based on tradition, _____, and _____ authority. (More Light on the Text)

COMMITTING TO THE WORD

19. Memorize and write verbatim 1 Corinthians 15:21. _____

_____

_____

_____

WALKING IN THE WORD

20. Paul explained the core of the Gospel message clearly and quickly to the Corinthians. How would you present the Gospel quickly—in a few sentences—to someone who had never heard it? _____

_____

_____

_____

"For this is the message that ye heard from the beginning, that we should love one another"
(1 John 3:11).

LOVE ONE ANOTHER

1 John 3:11–24

Use with Bible Study Guide 7

WORDS, PHRASES, DEFINITIONS

Define each of the following words as it relates to the lesson:

1. Cain _____

2. Agape _____

3. Truth _____

4. The wicked one _____

5. Bowels _____

6. John (the Apostle) _____

7. Abide _____

8. Narcissistic _____

9. Perceive _____

10. Condemn _____

JUMP-STARTING THE LESSON

11. What did Marcy do with the money she had saved for a new bicycle? _____ (In Focus)

12. Love is more than _____; it involves _____. (In Focus)

UNDERSTANDING THE LESSON

13. John asks Christians to love in _____ . (Focal Verses)

    a. word and deed

    b. deed and truth

    c. the name of Jesus

14. Cain was a _____ of the soil while his brother was a _____ of sheep. (The People, Places, and Times)

15. Jesus gave His disciples a "new commandment" that they should love _____ . (The People, Places, and Times)

16. Jesus made it very clear that love was a _____ of God's blessing, not a _____ for it. (Background)

17. There is no greater witness of Christ to the saved or the unsaved than _____ . (In Depth)
    a. Reciting Scripture without explaining it
    b. Wearing Christian jewelry
    c. Threatening them with fire and brimstone
    d. Expressing the love of God

18. A nominal Christian who does not demonstrate the gift of prophecy has not embarked on his spiritual journey; that person is still in a static state of death. (More Light On The Text)
    TRUE   FALSE

COMMITTING TO THE WORD

19. Memorize and write verbatim 1 John 3:16. _____

_____

_____

_____

WALKING IN THE WORD

20. John addresses the church and tells them to "love one another." Does this mean Christians must love everyone else or does this verse only apply to people within the church? _____

_____

_____

_____

> "Whosoever believeth that Jesus is the Christ is born of God: and every one that loveth him that begat loveth him also that is begotten of him" (1 John 5:1).

BELIEVE GOD'S LOVE

1 John 4:13–5:5

Use with Bible Study Guide 8

WORDS, PHRASES, DEFINITIONS

Define each of the following words as it relates to the lesson:

1. Day of Judgment _____

2. Johannine _____

3. Grievous _____

4. Fear _____

5. Overcome _____

6. Confess _____

7. Perfect _____

8. Torment _____

9. Believe _____

10. Boldness _____

JUMP-STARTING THE LESSON

11. What did Deidra finally do to stop Ricky's unwanted attention? _____ (In Focus)

12. If we cannot love our fellow Christian who is _____, we cannot love God who is _____. (In Focus)

UNDERSTANDING THE LESSON

13. Perfect love and _____ are mutually exclusive. (Focal Verses)

    a. Hate

    b. Fear

    c. Evil

14. John wrote five books of the Bible: _____, _____, _____, _____, and Revelation. (The People, Places, and Times)

15. The Old Testament and the New Testament understanding of the Day of Judgment are exactly the same. (The People, Places, and Times)

    TRUE   FALSE

16. In his first epistle, John talks at length about how _____ is evidence of a person's relationship to God. (Background)

17. How we treat each other is in _____ with how much we love God. (In Depth)

18. John connects the idea of Christian love with _____ . (More Light on the Text)

    a. Faith

    b. Obedience

    c. Fearlessness

    d. All the above

COMMITTING TO THE WORD

19. Memorize and write verbatim 1 John 5:3. _____
    _____
    _____
    _____

WALKING IN THE WORD

20. Review 1 John 4:20 and compare it with Matthew 5:21–22. How seriously do you take loving fellow believers? _____
    _____
    _____
    _____

"Look to yourselves, that we lose not those things which we have wrought, but that we receive a full reward" (2 John 8).

WATCH OUT FOR DECEIVERS!

2 John

Use with Bible Study Guide 9

WORDS, PHRASES, DEFINITIONS

Define each of the following words as it relates to the lesson:

1. Chosen lady _____

2. Elder _____

3. "Walking in truth" _____

4. Deceiver _____

5. Transgress _____

6. Doctrine _____

7. God speed _____

8. Beseech _____

9. Docetist _____

10. Antichrist _____

JUMP-STARTING THE LESSON

11. What made Trina not want a second date? _____ (In Focus)

12. Christians learn the value of walking in _____ and in _____. (In Focus)

UNDERSTANDING THE LESSON

13. The commandment that John gives his readers is _____. (Focal Verses)

    a. That we love Jesus

    b. That we renounce Satan

    c. That we love one another

    d. That we evangelize the nations

14. The "chosen lady" refers either to a matron who hosted a house church or the churches themselves located in _____ . (The People, Places, and Times)

15. The New Testament church based its practice of appointing elders on the Old Testament Jewish tradition. (The People, Places, and Times)

      TRUE   FALSE

16. The deceivers John wrote against in this letter believed Jesus was not fully divine. (Background)

      TRUE   FALSE

17. Which of these was not mentioned as a common outcome of fallacious doctrine? (In Depth)

    a. Disregard for the welfare of others

    b. Final departure from the faith

    c. Acceptance of sin

    d. Moral irresponsibility

18. To _____ in the full humanity and divinity of Christ and His redemptive mission, and to demonstrate _____, is proof of the new birth. (More Light on the Text)

COMMITTING TO THE WORD

19. Memorize and write verbatim 2 John 6._____

_____

_____

_____

WALKING IN THE WORD

20. Why is having the right doctrine so closely linked with the command to love one another? _____

_____

_____

_____

"We therefore ought to receive such, that we might be fellowhelpers to the truth"
(3 John 8).

COWORKERS WITH THE TRUTH

3 John

Use with Bible Study Guide 10

WORDS, PHRASES, DEFINITIONS

Define each of the following words as it relates to the lesson:

1. Gentiles _____

2. Gaius _____

3. Fellowhelpers _____

4. Prosper _____

5. Truth _____

6. Diotrephes _____

7. "Bring forward" _____

8. Follow _____

9. "For his name's sake" _____

10. Preeminence _____

JUMP-STARTING THE LESSON

11. How did the two ministers view their payment for preaching? _____ (In Focus)

12. We are called to show _____ to God's servants in whatever way we can. (In Focus)

UNDERSTANDING THE LESSON

13. What did the believers walk in that caused John to rejoice? (Focal Verses)

  a. Peace

  b. Love

  c. Truth

  d. Holiness

14. Gaius may have been ordained as the _____ of Pergamum. (The People, Places, and Times)

15. Diotrephes loved to show believers hospitality. (The People, Places, and Times)
       TRUE   FALSE

16. John was both a _____ and _____ elder. (Background)

17. To call oneself a Christian yet refuse hospitality to believers is to commit a _____ sin. (In Depth)

18. John's desire for believers to be prosperous and in good health can be placed in what category? (More Light on the Text)
    a. A promise
    b. A statement
    c. A greeting/general well wishes
    d. All the above

COMMITTING TO THE WORD
19. Memorize and write verbatim 3 John 4._____
_____
_____
_____

WALKING IN THE WORD
20. Hospitality needs to be a high priority for believers. How can you begin to show hospitality in your daily life? _____
_____
_____
_____

"But the manifestation of the Spirit is given to every man to profit withal" (1 Corinthians 12:7).

GIFTS OF THE SPIRIT

1 Corinthians 12:1–11

Use with Bible Study Guide 11

WORDS, PHRASES, DEFINITIONS
Define each of the following words as it relates to the lesson:

1. Administrations _____

2. Operations _____

3. Idols _____

4. Ignorant _____

5. Spiritual gifts _____

6. Knowledge _____

7. Wisdom _____

8. Miracles _____

9. Tongues _____

10. Lord _____

JUMP-STARTING THE LESSON

11. What convicted Joe about his lack of contributing to the good of the church? _____
_____ (In Focus)

12. We are called to _____ to the church through the spiritual gifts that God has given each of us. (In Focus)

UNDERSTANDING THE LESSON

13. What is not included in Paul's list of spiritual gifts? (Focal Verses)
    a. Word of wisdom
    b. Faith

c. Cooking

d. Discernment

14. Corinth was a city that was full of _____ . (The People, Places, and Times)

15. In Corinth, Paul preached to a mostly Gentile audience. (The People, Places, and Times)
    TRUE   FALSE

16. The Corinthian church had been wrapped up in all kinds of _____ and
    _____ practices. (Background)

17. God grants many _____ spiritual gifts, which operate and _____
    the body of Christ in different ways. (In Depth)

18. What cannot come from the lips of someone influenced by the Holy Spirit? (More Light on the Text)
    a. Jesus is Lord
    b. To live is Christ
    c. Let us eat and drink, for tomorrow we die
    d. Accursed be Jesus

COMMITTING TO THE WORD

19. Memorize and write verbatim 1 Corinthians 12:1. _____
    _____
    _____

WALKING IN THE WORD

20. Paul gives a list of spiritual gifts. Do you know which ones the Lord has given you? How do you use
    those gifts for the common good of the church? _____
    _____
    _____
    _____

> "For by one Spirit are we all baptized into one body, whether we be Jews or Gentiles, whether we be bond or free; and have been all made to drink into one Spirit" (1 Corinthians 12:13).

THE SPIRIT CREATES ONE BODY

1 Corinthians 12:14–31

Use with Bible Study Guide 12

WORDS, PHRASES, DEFINITIONS

Define each of the following words as it relates to the lesson:

1. Tempered _____

2. Schism _____

3. Helps _____

4. Governments _____

5. Apostle _____

6. "Covet earnestly" _____

7. Comeliness _____

8. Suffer _____

9. Feeble _____

10. Excellent _____

JUMP-STARTING THE LESSON

11. Why did Mrs. Parker hide her gift of singing? _____ (In Focus)

12. We must never forget that we all have a _____ to play in the _____ of Christ. (In Focus)

UNDERSTANDING THE LESSON

13. According to Paul, what should not be found in the body of Christ? (Focal Verses)

    a. Alcohol

    b. Freedom

    c. Schism

    d. Unclean spirits

14. The gift of helps is the ability to aid, _____, and support others. (The People, Places, and Times)

15. The gift of governments is the ability to run for political office. (The People, Places, and Times)
    TRUE   FALSE

16. Each and every member _____ to the health and _____ of the whole body. (Background)

17. Paul uses _____ questions to state the fact that the church is one body. (In Depth)

18. What does Paul say we need to do in regards to the best gifts? (More Light on the Text)
    a. Ignore them
    b. Honor those who have them
    c. Covet them earnestly
    d. Practice them

COMMITTING TO THE WORD

19. Memorize and write verbatim 1 Corinthians 12:31. _____
    _____
    _____
    _____

WALKING IN THE WORD

20. God wants us all to work together as one body. How can you contribute to the unity of your local church through your spiritual gift? _____
    _____
    _____
    _____

"What is it then? I will pray with the spirit, and I will pray with the understanding also: I will sing with the spirit, and I will sing with the understanding also" (1 Corinthians 14:15).

GIFT OF LANGUAGES

Acts 2:1–7, 12; 1 Corinthians 14:13–19

Use with Bible Study Guide 13

WORDS, PHRASES, DEFINITIONS
Define each of the following words as it relates to the lesson:

1. Utterance _____

2. Unlearned _____

3. Tongues _____

4. Pentecost _____

5. "Was fully come" _____

6. Confounded _____

7. Amazed _____

8. Unfruitful _____

9. Bless _____

10. Ten thousand _____

JUMP-STARTING THE LESSON

11. What caused Karen to feel uncomfortable when visiting Mark's church? _____

    (In Focus)

12. God has given us the privilege and _____ to communicate _____

    for the benefit of others, especially unbelievers. (In Focus)

UNDERSTANDING THE LESSON

13. How many intelligible words would Paul rather speak than ten thousand in an unknown tongue?

    (Focal Verses)

    a. Ten

b. Thirty

c. Five

d. One hundred

14. The phenomenon of speaking in _____ is prominent in the book of Acts and refers to the ability to speak in a known or an _____ language. (The People, Places, and Times)

15. Pentecost was when the Israelites remembered Abraham leaving his country for Canaan. (The People, Places, and Times)
       TRUE   FALSE

16. Some had _____ themselves on speaking in tongues. (Background)

17. Paul _____ the Corinthians that whoever speaks in tongues needs to _____ for interpretation. (In Depth)

18. What Greek word is translated as "speaking in tongues"? (More Light on the Text)

a. Koinonia

b. Laleo

c. Glossolalia

d. All the above

COMMITTING TO THE WORD

19. Memorize and write verbatim 1 Corinthians 14:19. _____

_____

_____

WALKING IN THE WORD

20. God prioritizes clear communication. How can you prioritize clear communication with regard to spiritual things? _____

_____

_____

"And now abideth faith, hope, and charity, these three; but the greatest of these is charity" (1 Corinthians 13:13).

THE GREATEST GIFT IS LOVE

1 Corinthians 13

Use with Bible Study Guide 14

WORDS, PHRASES, DEFINITIONS

Define each of the following words as it relates to the lesson:

1. Charity _____
2. Hope _____
3. Corinth _____
4. "Suffereth long" _____
5. Vaunteth _____
6. Perfect _____
7. Glass _____
8. Envieth _____
9. "Puffed up" _____
10. Endureth _____

JUMP-STARTING THE LESSON

11. What provoked the old woman next door to invite Alison and Christie inside? _____

_____ (In Focus)

12. Love brings out the _____ in others and always _____ to do good.

    (In Focus)

UNDERSTANDING THE LESSON

13. Love is more important than which activity? (Focal Verses)

    a. Speaking in tongues

    b. Prophesying

c. Giving to the poor

d. All of the above

14. The city of Corinth was located in the country of _____. (The People, Places, and Times)

15. The city of Corinth was known for its godly behavior and morality. (The People, Places, and Times)

   TRUE   FALSE

16. Paul wrote 1 Corinthians while he was living and ministering in the city of _____. (Background)

17. Spiritual gifts are nothing without love; they can even be _____ when not practiced in love. (In Depth)

18. What is the lifeblood of the body of Christ? (More Light on the Text)

   a. Faith

   b. Obedience

   c. Fearlessness

   d. Charity

COMMITTING TO THE WORD

19. Memorize and write verbatim 1 Corinthians 13:1. _____

   _____

   _____

   _____

WALKING IN THE WORD

20. Agape love seeks to bring out the best in others. How can you bring out the best in others in your daily life? _____

   _____

   _____

   _____

"*Thus saith the LORD ... because they have despised the law of the LORD, and have not kept His commandments, and their lies have caused them to err, after the which their fathers have walked*" (Amos 2:4).

JUDGMENT ON ISRAEL AND JUDAH

Amos 2:4–8

Use with Bible Study Guide 1

WORDS, PHRASES, DEFINITIONS

Define each of the following words as it relates to the lesson:

1. Transgression _____

2. Despise _____

3. Tekoa _____

4. Slavery _____

5. "For three transgressions and for four" _____

6. Lies _____

7. Palaces _____

8. Pant _____

9. Profane _____

10. Righteous _____

JUMP-STARTING THE LESSON

11. How did Tony help Kodjo to get a new lease agreement from his landlord? _____

_____ (In Focus)

12. God's _____ of injustice causes us to _____ against it in our

own community. (In Focus)

UNDERSTANDING THE LESSON

13. What main sins did Judah and Israel commit? (Focal Verses)

    a. Idolatry

    b. Gossip

c. Social injustice

d. Both a. and c.

14. Amos was originally from a town in _____ named Tekoa. (The People, Places, and Times)

15. Slavery in the ancient Near East was similar to the slavery of African Americans. (The People, Places, and Times)

     TRUE   FALSE

16. Amos was a _____ and tended sycamore _____. (Background)

17. Israel's _____ of God's law resulted in horrible abuses against its people. (In Depth)

18. The word "lies" is a reference to what sin? (More Light on the Text)

a. False witness

b. Witchcraft

c. Idolatry

d. All the above

COMMITTING TO THE WORD

19. Memorize and write verbatim Amos 2:6. _____

_____

_____

_____

WALKING IN THE WORD

20. God desires justice in our communities. What are some injustices you can address in your community? _____

_____

_____

_____

"But let judgment run down as waters and righteousness as a mighty stream" (Amos 5:24).

GOD IS NOT FOOLED

Amos 5:14–15, 18–27

Use with Bible Study Guide 2

WORDS, PHRASES, DEFINITIONS

Define each of the following words as it relates to the lesson:

1. Gracious _____

2. Righteousness _____

3. Feast Days _____

4. Sikkuth _____

5. Kaiwan _____

6. "The Day of the Lord" _____

7. Assemblies _____

8. Meat offerings _____

9. Burnt offerings _____

10. Stream _____

JUMP-STARTING THE LESSON

11. What did Jenna do to help the woman get her car back from the shop? _____ (In Focus)

12. God desires that we would _____ justice and _____ evil.
    (In Focus)

UNDERSTANDING THE LESSON

13. What did the Lord say that He despised? (Focal Verses)

    a. Feast days

    b. Viols

    c. Assemblies

    d. Both a. and c.

14. There were three major _____ days in the nation of Israel. (The People, Places, and Times)

15. Sikkuth and Kaiwan are the names of gods that represented the planet Saturn. (The People, Places, and Times)

           TRUE   FALSE

16. The Israelites were known to visit _____ temples in Bethel, Gilgal, and Beersheba. (Background)

17. The Lord desires a _____ daily flow of justice and righteousness. (In Depth)

18. The Lord would not accept which of these things from Israel? (More Light on the Text)

    a. Peace offerings

    b. Burnt offerings

    c. Grain offerings

    d. All the above

COMMITTING TO THE WORD

19. Memorize and write verbatim Amos 5:14. _____

_____

_____

_____

WALKING IN THE WORD

20. The Lord wants us to seek good and avoid evil. How can you seek good and avoid evil when it comes to social injustice? _____

_____

_____

_____

"Shall horses run upon the rock? will one plow there with oxen? for ye have turned judgment into gall, and the fruit of righteousness into hemlock" (Amos 6:12).

REBUKED FOR SELFISHNESS

Amos 6:4–8, 11–14

Use with Bible Study Guide 3

WORDS, PHRASES, DEFINITIONS

Define each of the following words as it relates to the lesson:

1. Chant _____

2. Afflict _____

3. Viols _____

4. Ointments _____

5. "Hamath to the River of the Wilderness" _____

6. "Pride of Jacob" _____

7. Abhor _____

8. Bowls _____

9. Joseph _____

10. Lo-Debar _____

JUMP-STARTING THE LESSON

11. What selfish thing did Michael do as he saw a young mother struggling to take her children to

    school? _____ (In Focus)

12. God invites us to _____ in ending the injustice that oppresses humanity. (In Focus)

UNDERSTANDING THE LESSON

13. What did the Israelites spend time doing instead of grieving over their sins? (Focal Verses)
    a. Buying and selling
    b. Following a false religion

c. Feasting and lounging

d. Helping other nations

14. Hamath to the river of the wilderness _____ the entirety of the undivided kingdom of Israel. (The People, Places, and Times)

15. Ointments were used to grease chariot wheels. (The People, Places, and Times)
      TRUE   FALSE

16. Those in leadership believed that Israel's cities were _____ to others because of their extravagant and materialistic luxuries. (Background)

17. Often when we experience an _____ in wealth, we forget about God and the plight of others. (In Depth)

18. What did Israel do to the cities of Lo-Debar and Karnaim? (More Light on the Text)
      a. Burned them down
      b. Sieged them
      c. Recaptured them
      d. All of the above

COMMITTING TO THE WORD

19. Memorize and write verbatim Amos 6:11. _____

_____

_____

_____

WALKING IN THE WORD

20. God despises our selfishness. How can we become generous and unselfish people toward those around us? _____

_____

_____

_____

"And he said, what seest thou? And I said, A basket of summer fruit. Then said the LORD unto me, The end is come upon my people of Israel; I will not again pass by them anymore" (Amos 8:2).

GOD WILL NEVER FORGET

Amos 8:1–6, 9–10

Use with Bible Study Guide 4

WORDS, PHRASES, DEFINITIONS

Define each of the following words as it relates to the lesson:

1. Sackcloth _____

2. Lamentation _____

3. Amos _____

4. New Moon _____

5. Summer fruit _____

6. Howling _____

7. "And it shall come to pass"_____

8. "Mourning of an only son" _____

9. "Made the ephah small and made the shekel great" _____

10. "Baldness on every head"_____

JUMP-STARTING THE LESSON

11. What was Monique thinking about as she left the store? _____
_____ (In Focus)

12. Those who practice _____ will face God's judgment. (In Focus)

UNDERSTANDING THE LESSON

13. What was the price of enslaving the poor and needy? (Focal Verses)

   a. Silver

   b. A pair of shoes

c. A lamb

d. Both a. and b.

14. The New Moon was a _____ held at the beginning of every lunar month. (The People, Places, and Times)

15. Amos ministered in Israel around 750 B.C. (The People, Places, and Times)
    TRUE   FALSE

16. The Lord gave Amos a series of _____ that described Israel's complete destruction. (Background)

17. Summer fruit was a _____ of Israel's impending judgment. (In Depth)

18. What days caused those who committed injustice to temporarily cease? (More Light on the Text)
    a. Day of Atonement and Passover
    b. New Moon and Sabbath
    c. Pentecost and the Feast of Booths
    d. All of the above

COMMITTING TO THE WORD

19. Memorize and write verbatim Amos 8:9. _____

_____

_____

_____

WALKING IN THE WORD

20. The Lord calls us to seek justice even in our commerce. How can you seek justice in your buying and spending and other business dealings? _____

_____

_____

_____

> "O thou that art named the house of Jacob, is the Spirit of the LORD straitened? are these his doings? do not my words do good to him that walketh uprightly?" (Micah 2:7).

No Rest for the Wicked

Micah 2:4–11

Use with Bible Study Guide 5

WORDS, PHRASES, DEFINITIONS

Define each of the following words as it relates to the lesson:

1. Parable _____

2. Prophesy _____

3. Micah _____

4. House of Jacob _____

5. Lamentation _____

6. Straitened _____

7. Rest _____

8. Polluted _____

9. "Cast the cord by lot" _____

10. "Men averse from war" _____

JUMP-STARTING THE LESSON

11. What caused Bill's stomach to churn and become nauseated? _____
_____ (In Focus)

12. We cannot _____ evil and wrongdoings in our communities. (In Focus)

UNDERSTANDING THE LESSON

13. What will the wicked landowners fail to have in the congregation of the Lord? (Focal Verses)

    a. One to cast the cord by lot

    b. A priest

c. A sacrifice

d. A judge

14. Micah's name means "Who is like _____ ?" (The People, Places, and Times)

15. A lamentation is a joyful song for special occasions. (The People, Places, and Times)

    TRUE   FALSE

16. Micah 2 begins with a _____ of the deeds of wealthy land barons and their wanton greed. (Background)

17. The people of _____ had no interest in Micah's _____ of judgment. (In Depth)

18. What will people do to the rich landowners when disaster comes? (More Light on the Text)

    a. Support them

    b. Steal from them

    c. Mock them

    d. All the above

COMMITTING TO THE WORD

19. Memorize and write verbatim Micah 2:11. _____

    _____

    _____

    _____

WALKING IN THE WORD

20. We cannot justify evil or wrongdoings in our lives or communities. How can we expose those who do evil and commit injustice? _____

    _____

    _____

    _____

No Tolerance for Corrupt Leaders and Prophets

"But truly I am full of power by the spirit of the LORD, and of judgment, and of might, to declare unto Jacob his transgression and to Israel his sin" (Micah 3:8).

Micah 3:5–12

Use with Bible Study Guide 6

WORDS, PHRASES, DEFINITIONS

Define each of the following words as it relates to the lesson:

1. Confounded _____

2. Equity _____

3. Heads _____

4. False prophets _____

5. Err _____

6. Bite _____

7. Divine _____

8. Judgment _____

9. Zion _____

10. Lean _____

JUMP-STARTING THE LESSON

11. How did Pastor Hindley handle Kim's questions about the discrepancies in the books? _____
_____ (In Focus)

12. Leaders should not _____ the interests of the people they are
positioned to support. (In Focus)

UNDERSTANDING THE LESSON

13. What is Micah filled with in order to declare the injustices of the leaders of Israel and Judah?
(Focal Verses)
a. Anger

b. Righteousness

c. Power by the Spirit of the Lord

d. The word of God

14. By the time of the _____, the heads were known for taking bribes and being partial to the rich. (The People, Places, and Times)

15. Prophets were evaluated by whether they spoke highly of other prophets. (The People, Places, and Times)

        TRUE   FALSE

16. The _____ empire was a very dominant and real threat to Jerusalem at Micah's time. (Background)

17. Micah says the leaders are attempting to _____ up the city but at the expense of the poor. (In Depth)

18. What are other definitions of shalom besides peace? (More Light on the Text)

a. Fun

b. Welfare

c. Prosperity

d. Both b. and c.

COMMITTING TO THE WORD

19. Memorize and write verbatim Micah 3:7._____

_____

_____

_____

WALKING IN THE WORD

20. Leaders should not abandon the interests of the people. How can you as a Christian hold your community leaders accountable? _____

_____

_____

_____

JUSTICE, LOVE, AND HUMILITY

"He hath shewed thee, O man, what is good; and what doth the LORD require of thee, but to do justly, to love mercy, and to walk humbly with thy God" (Micah 6:8).

Micah 6:3–8

Use with Bible Study Guide 7

WORDS, PHRASES, DEFINITIONS

Define each of the following words as it relates to the lesson:

1. Redeem _____

2. Mercy _____

3. Balaam _____

4. Human sacrifice _____

5. Wearied _____

6. Testify _____

7. Bowing _____

8. "Fruit of my body" _____

9. Justice _____

10. Humbly _____

JUMP-STARTING THE LESSON

11. What did Edward realize about his business after talking to Quincy, his first partner? _____
_____ (In Focus)

12. God _____ that we would respond to His blessings in our life. (In Focus)

UNDERSTANDING THE LESSON

13. What does the Lord not require of His people? (Focal Verses)
    a. Justice
    b. Humility

c. Perfection

d. Mercy

14. Balaam was highly _____ among the Midianites and had great power and influence. (The People, Places, and Times)

15. There is some evidence of child sacrifice in ancient Greek and Egyptian culture. (The People, Places, and Times)
          TRUE   FALSE

16. Micah's prophecy begins with a general announcement to _____ and _____. (Background)

17. The inward condition of one's _____ is of more concern to God than outward religiosity. (In Depth)

18. What two cities are references to Israel's conquest of the land? (More Light on the Text)
a. Jerusalem and Samaria
b. Shittim and Gilgal
c. Jericho and Beersheba
d. All the above

COMMITTING TO THE WORD

19. Memorize and write verbatim Micah 6:4. _____
_____
_____
_____

WALKING IN THE WORD

20. God requires justice, mercy, and faithfulness to Him. How are you exhibiting these things in your life? _____
_____
_____
_____

"*Who is a God like unto thee, that pardoneth iniquity, and passeth by the transgression of the remnant of his heritage? he retaineth not his anger for ever, because he delighteth in mercy*" (Micah 7:18).

GOD SHOWS CLEMENCY

Micah 7:14–20

Use with Bible Study Guide 8

WORDS, PHRASES, DEFINITIONS
Define each of the following words as it relates to the lesson:

1. Remnant _____

2. Iniquity _____

3. Bashan _____

4. Gilead _____

5. Staff _____

6. "Lick the dust like a serpent" _____

7. Compassion _____

8. "Dwell soliarily in the woods" _____

9. Delighteth _____

10. Pardoneth _____

JUMP-STARTING THE LESSON

11. What allowed Lin to forgive the contractor for his failure? _____
_____ (In Focus)

12. While _____ are essential to maintaining order, they are not always _____ to maintaining a relationship. (In Focus)

UNDERSTANDING THE LESSON

13. What animals does Micah use to describe the surrounding nations? (Focal Verses)
    a. Foxes
    b. Snakes

c. Worms

d. Both b. and c.

14. The area east of the Jordan river was divided into three parts: the plain, Gilead, and _____. (The People, Places, and Times)

15. Gilead became synonymous with God's healing power. (The People, Places, and Times)

      TRUE   FALSE

16. Micah begins chapter 7 _____ the evil and injustice done in Judah. (Background)

17. Micah _____ in the covenant between his ancestors and God. (In Depth)

18. During what time did God show Israel marvelous things? (More Light on the Text)

a. When they crowned David king

b. When they had judges ruling the land

c. When they came out of Egypt

d. All of the above

COMMITTING TO THE WORD

19. Memorize and write verbatim Micah 7:19._____

_____

_____

_____

WALKING IN THE WORD

20. Micah shows us that God is a God of mercy and forgiveness. What picture comes to mind when you describe God? _____

_____

_____

_____

"And the Redeemer shall come to Zion, and unto them that turn from transgression in Jacob, saith the LORD" (Isaiah 59:20).

OUR REDEEMER COMES

Isaiah 59:15b–21

Use with Bible Study Guide 9

WORDS, PHRASES, DEFINITIONS

Define each of the following words as it relates to the lesson:

1. Recompense _____

2. Intercessor _____

3. Islands _____

4. Redeemer _____

5. Fear _____

6. Arm _____

7. Sustain _____

8. Cloak _____

9. Fury _____

10. Zeal _____

JUMP-STARTING THE LESSON

11. Why did Juan tell Mya not to put too much faith in the company's discrimination policies? _____
_____ (In Focus)

12. We can _____ with God to work for a renewed society. (In Focus)

UNDERSTANDING THE LESSON

13. What is not a piece of the armor that God will put on to bring justice? (Focal Verses)

   a. Helmet

   b. Breastplate

c. Sword

d. Cloak

14. For the Israelite, "the coastlands" such as Greece or Italy _____ the ends of the earth. (The People, Places, and Times)

15. A redeemer was one who took revenge for the murder of a deceased relative. (The People, Places, and Times)

        TRUE   FALSE

16. Hezekiah led a rebellion against the _____ empire. (Background)

17. Isaiah makes it clear that those who _____ justice and truth will be held accountable. (In Depth)

18. How will the Lord come when He exacts vengeance on His enemies? (More Light on the Text)

a. Like an eagle in flight

b. Like a flashing sharp sword

c. Like a pent up flood

d. Like a roaring lion

COMMITTING TO THE WORD

19. Memorize and write verbatim Isaiah 59:16. _____

_____

_____

WALKING IN THE WORD

20. God wants us to partner with his cause of justice. How can you become involved in God's cause of justice in your daily life? _____

_____

_____

_____

> "Thus saith the LORD of hosts, the God of Israel, Amend your ways and your doings, and I will cause you to dwell in this place" (Jeremiah 7:3).

A CHOICE TO BE JUST

Jeremiah 7:1–15

Use with Bible Study Guide 10

WORDS, PHRASES, DEFINITIONS
Define each of the following words as it relates to the lesson:

1. Amend _____

2. Abomination _____

3. Shiloh _____

4. The temple in Jerusalem _____

5. Trust _____

6. "The land" _____

7. Thoroughly execute judgment _____

8. Delivered _____

9. Den _____

10. "Rising up early" _____

JUMP-STARTING THE LESSON

11. What did Jeff ask God to do after he realized his life didn't match his profession of faith? _____ _____ (In Focus)

12. Jeremiah warns the people of Judah that their _____ are evil and they need to _____ their ways or face judgment. (In Focus)

UNDERSTANDING THE LESSON

13. What caused the people to believe that they were safe? (Focal Verses)
    a. Their righteousness
    b. God's promises

c. Their military

d. The temple

14. Shiloh was a place in Israel where the _____ resided. (The People, Places, and Times)

15. The people believed that God resided in the temple. (The People, Places, and Times)

        TRUE   FALSE

16. Judah fell to the _____ less than 25 years after Jeremiah issued his sermon of warning and hope. (Background)

17. The people had put their _____ in the temple of the Lord instead of the Lord of the temple. (In Depth)

18. What did Jeremiah liken the temple to because of the people's sins? (More Light on the Text)

a. A house of wickedness

b. A tower of destruction

c. A den of robbers

d. All of the above

COMMITTING TO THE WORD

19. Memorize and write verbatim Jeremiah 7:8. _____

_____

_____

_____

WALKING IN THE WORD

20. The people trusted in the temple and not in the Lord. How can we avoid putting our trust in things other than God? _____

_____

_____

_____

> "Repent, and turn from your sins! Don't let them destroy you! Put all your rebellion behind you, and find yourselves a new heart and a new spirit" (from Ezekiel 18:30–31).

A CALL TO REPENTANCE

Ezekiel 18:1–13, 31–32

Use with Bible Study Guide 11

WORDS, PHRASES, DEFINITIONS

Define each of the following words as it relates to the lesson:

1. Soul _____

2. Turn _____

3. Proverbs _____

4. Usury _____

5. Fathers _____

6. Heart _____

7. "Sour grapes" _____

8. Spirit _____

9. Pleasure _____

10. Live _____

JUMP-STARTING THE LESSON

11. What did Philip decide was the best way out of his situation? _____ (In Focus)

12. Ezekiel warns the people of Judah of approaching danger and pleads with them to take _____
_____ for their actions, repent, and live. (Focal Verses)

UNDERSTANDING THE LESSON

13. According to the Israelite proverb, what caused the children's teeth to be set on edge? (Focal Verses)

    a. Loud noise

    b. Goat's milk

c. Barley

d. Sour grapes

14. Proverbs are a way of _____ wisdom or real-life truth. (The People, Places, and Times)

15. The Israelites could not charge interest to strangers. (The People, Places, and Times)
    TRUE   FALSE

16. Ezekiel's sermon in this lesson was preached to an audience living in exile in _____. (Background)

17. Each person is _____ for his own actions. (In Depth)

18. What does the Lord not take pleasure in? (More Light on the Text)
    a. The death of him that dieth
    b. Unconfessed sin
    c. Empty worship songs
    d. All of the above

COMMITTING TO THE WORD

19. Memorize and write verbatim Ezekiel 18:4. _____
_____
_____
_____

WALKING IN THE WORD

20. God has given us responsibility for our own lives. What areas in your life do you need to assume responsibility for? _____
_____
_____
_____

GOD DEMANDS JUSTICE

Zechariah 7:8–14

> "Thus speaketh the Lord of hosts, saying, Execute true judgment, and show mercy, and compassions every man to his brother: and not oppress the widow, nor the fatherless, nor the stranger, nor the poor, and let none of you imagine evil against his brother in your heartt" (Zechariah 7:9-10).

Use with Bible Study Guide 12

WORDS, PHRASES, DEFINITIONS
Write the definition of the following words as they relate to the lesson.

1. Wrath _____

2. Desolate _____

3. Zechariah _____

4. Post-Exilic Period _____

5. Whirlwind _____

6. Oppress _____

7. Hearken _____

8. Adamant stone _____

9. Mercy and Compassions _____

10. "Stopped their ears" _____

JUMP-STARTING THE LESSON

11. What did John mean when he said he wanted to pay for food he can trust? _____ _____(In Focus)

12. We may not be able to change the world _____ but we must start with _____ God's voice. (In Focus)

UNDERSTANDING THE LESSON

13. What did the Lord use to scatter His people "among all the nations whom they knew not"? (Focal Verses)

    a. An army

b. Angels

c. A whirlwind

d. A famine

14. Zechariah was most likely a young _____ when he first began to prophesy. (The People, Places, and Times)

15. The Israelites made their hearts as an adamant stone (The People, Places, and Times)
        TRUE   FALSE

16. Zechariah prophesied during a time of great upheaval in the _____ Empire. (Background)

17. Zechariah recalls the people's _____ disobedience (In Depth)

18. What does it mean to pull away the shoulder? (More Light on the Text)

a. To dance

b. To hide your sin

c. To turn your back

d. All of the above

COMMITTING TO THE WORD

19. Memorize and write verbatim Zechariah 7:11. _____

_____

_____

_____

WALKING IN THE WORD

20. God wants His people to hear His voice. What is the Lord saying to you in regards to pursuing justice and compassion? _____

_____

_____

_____

> "Even from the days of your fathers ye are gone away from mine ordinances, and have not kept them. Return unto me, and I will return unto you, saith the LORD of hosts. But ye said, Wherein shall we return?" (Malachi 3:7).

RETURN TO A JUST GOD

Malachi 3:1–10

Use with Bible Study Guide 13

WORDS, PHRASES, DEFINITIONS

Define each of the following words as it relates to the lesson:

1. Purge _____

2. Ordinance _____

3. Refiner _____

4. Fuller _____

5. Hireling _____

6. Tithes and offerings _____

7. Prepare _____

8. Abide _____

9. Soap _____

10. Curse _____

JUMP-STARTING THE LESSON

11. What was the main reason for Stanley's refusal to give? _____ (In Focus)

12. Faithfulness to a _____ God can be shown in our giving. (In Focus)

UNDERSTANDING THE LESSON

13. What will the messenger of the covenant do when he comes? (Focal Verses)

    a. Announce the Lord's coming

    b. Bring the sacrifices

    c. Sit as a refiner

    d. Defeat God's enemies

14. The refiner's tools were a _____ or furnace and a _____ or a blowpipe. (The People, Places, and Times)

15. A hireling was a part-time worker. (The People, Places, and Times)
           TRUE   FALSE

16. Malachi was written during the _____ period. (Background)

17. Although they demanded justice, they _____ God by not giving the tithes of their crops and herds. (In Depth)

18. What does the Lord promise to do when His people return to them? (More Light on the Text)
    a. Save them
    b. Bless them
    c. Return to them
    d. All the above

COMMITTING TO THE WORD

19. Memorize and write verbatim Malachi 3:6. _____

_____

_____

_____

WALKING IN THE WORD

20. Our faithfulness to God is shown in our giving. How is this applied in your daily life? _____

_____

_____

_____

ANSWER KEY

ANSWER KEY TO LESSON 1

1. Heap: a mound on which a city had previously stood
2. Engaged: to stand with certainty alongside someone, as a lender stands with a debtor assured that the debt will be paid
3. Captivity: exile or ill fortune
4. Nobles: leading men or rulers
5. Governor: king or one who exercises authority over others
6. Jacob's tents: nomadic dwelling; a symbol of wilderness life of Abraham, Isaac, and Jacob
7. Jeremiah: the weeping prophet
8. Judah: located between the Mediterranean and Dead Sea, in southern Palestine
9. Aforetime: from a former or past time
10. Congregation: assembly
11. alone
12. punished, redeeming, restoring
13. people, God
14. c. 19
15. e. 587 B.C.
16. Shiloh, Philistines
17. Jerusalem, former
18. Daniel, repentant
19. "And you shall be my people, and I will be your God" (Jeremiah 30:22, KJV).
20. Answers will vary.

ANSWER KEY TO LESSON 2

1. Covenant: a political and financial agreement with signs and pledges by both parties
2. Heart: the seat of the affections, intellect, and memory
3. Hosts: an organized army for service or battle
4. Babylonian Captivity: the period in biblical history when the people of Judah were defeated and taken away by the powerful nation of Babylonia
5. Anathoth: Jeremiah's hometown, a priestly community belonging to the tribe of Benjamin
6. "I took them by the hand: parental approach God uses toward Israel
7. Ordinances: limits, enactments, something prescribed
8. Divideth: to cause to rest
9. Seed: descendants, offspring, posterity
10. Brake: make void, or annul
11. Bill thanked God for giving him Lauren and allowing him to renew their covenant of marriage.
12. repeatedly, renew
13. forgive, remember
14. useful
15. c. Both of the above
16. e. Anathoth
17. neighbor, know
18. hearts; stone
19. "But this shall be the covenant that I will make with the house of Israel; After those days, saith the LORD, I will put my law in their inward parts, and write it in their hearts; and will be their God, and they shall be my people" (Jeremiah 31:33, KJV).
20. Answers will vary.

ANSWER KEY TO LESSON 3

1. Besieged: encircle and enclose a fortified area as a military strategy
2. Redemption: reclamation of inheritance or family members from servitude or difficulties
3. Zedekiah: last king of Judah and son of King Josiah
4. Babylonia: a tremendously wealthy and powerful kingdom between the Tigris and Euphrates rivers in southern Mesopotamia
5. Prophet: one who serves as medium of communication between human and divine worlds
6. Nebuchadnezzar: king of Babylonia
7. Hanameel: Jeremiah's cousin who sold him property
8. Law of redemption: the right of the closest relative to purchase family property
9. Visit: to punish (with death)
10. Shekel of silver: five dollars in 2010 USD
11. By buying a house
12. dire, hopeful
13. hope, prophetic
14. True
15. False
16. prophets, past, present, and future
17. proposition, land
18. Hanameel, two
19. Hosts, houses, vineyards, possessed
20. Answers will vary.

ANSWER KEY TO LESSON 4

1. Iniquity: sin or wickedness often with the focus on the guilt or liability incurred and the punishment to follow
2. Prosperity: peace, safety, well-being, and wholeness
3. Reveal: to uncover
4. Chaldea: another name for Neo-Babylonia
5. LORD: translated from Hebrew word Yahweh
6. Knowest: to understand
7. Mounts: siege ramps
8. Peace: welfare, health, prosperity
9. Truth: faithfulness, reliableness
10. Pardon: release or forgive
11. Forgive her and turn her life around
12. willing, restoration
13. restore, rebuild
14. e. Pakistan
15. c. Babylonia
16. Yahweh, promise
17. restore, rightful
18. inhabitants, occupied
19. "Behold, I will bring it health and cure, and I will cure them, and will reveal unto them the abundance of peace and truth" (Jeremiah 33:6, KJV).
20. Answers will vary.

ANSWER KEY TO LESSON 5

1. Vision: oracle, prophecy, divine communication
2. Faith: firmness, faithfulness, steadfastness
3. Habakkuk: a prophet of the late seventh century B.C.
4. Reproved: to be corrected
5. Tables: large wooden tablets
6. Hind: deer or gazelle
7. Stringed instruments: lyre or harp
8. Proud: arrogant or haughty
9. Tower: watchtower or siege enclosure
10. Tarry/Be delayed: to wait or remain behind after the appointed time
11. faith, care
12. done, doing, do
13. trust, suffering

14. True

15. e. Josiah

16. assurance, timing

17. separate, righteous, wicked

18. faith, faithfulness

19. "Behold, his soul which is lifted up is not upright in him: but the just shall live by faith" (Habakkuk 2:4, KJV).

20. Answers will vary.

ANSWER KEY TO LESSON 6

1. Reproach: to insult, shame, humiliate, be ashamed

2. Latter Day: following, subsequent, last of time

3. Redeemer: a person's nearest living kin who might save their next of kin from slavery or poverty

4. Job: a righteous man of Uz tested by God

5. Break: to crush into powder

6. Erred: having committed a minor sin in ignorance

7. Overthrown: to bend or pervert someone's cause

8. Reins: KJV translation for kidneys, the seat of emotions

9. Knowing that she would see the Lord one day

10. hope, His redemption

11. flesh

12. e. Uz

13. False

14. children, health

15. hunter

16. redeemer

17. ten, idiom

18. vindicate, sins

19. "And though after my skin worms destroy this body; yet in my flesh shall I see God" (Job 19:26, KJV).

20. Answers will vary.

ANSWER KEY TO LESSON 7

1. Almighty: powerful

2. Grave: realm of the dead

3. Drought: hated or persecuted one

4. Pledge: security given for future payment

5. Uz: poetic name for Edom

6. Sheaf: bundle of grain

7. Winepress: where grapes were squeezed and bruised to make wine

8. Entreateth evil: do evil

9. Drought: dryness

10. Pluck: snatch, strip off

11. By helping him get a job and a place to stay.

12. wicked, justice

13. injustice

14. c. A widow's clothing

15. True

16. Eliphaz

17. ultimate, wrongs

18. theodicy

19. "And if it be not so now, who will make me a liar, and make my speech nothing worth?" (Job 24:25, KJV).

20. Answers will vary.

ANSWER KEY TO LESSON 8

1. Abhor: to reject, despise, refuse

2. Burnt offering: sacrifice that is entirely burned

3. Dust and ashes: to sit and lie in dust and ashes as a sign of repentance and humiliation

4. Eliphaz, Bildad, Zophar: Job's friends who mourned with him for seven days after his loss

5. Repent: to sigh and breathe strongly with a sense of sorrow

6. Seven bulls and seven rams: a sacrifice signify-

ing complete atonement

7. Hideth: God's grand designs for the universe being concealed from us

8. Jemima: dove; Job's daughter

9. Kezia: cinnamon; Job's daughter

10. Kerenhappuch: expensive black eye makeup; Job's daughter

11. A mortgage assistance program reduced her mortgage and offered financial assistance.

12. rewarded

13. double

14. False

15. seven

16. questions, human

17. friends, bad advice

18. holy, sinful

19. "I have heard of thee by the hearing of the ear: but now mine eye seeth thee" (Job 42:5, KJV).

20. Answers will vary.

ANSWER KEY TO LESSON 9

1. Glory: abundance, splendor, reputation

2. Abominations: disgusting things in a ritual or ethical sense

3. Inner court: separate area of the temple reserved only for priests

4. Chebar river: a river that ran through the land of the Chaldeans

5. East: first or at the beginning

6. Parousia: Greek for presence or coming

7. Dwell: rest, reside, inhabit

8. Whoredom: idolatry

9. Defile: profane and treat with disrespect

10. Threshold: timber that lies under a door

11. The empty pews and the sanctuary

12. everywhere, presence

13. dwell

14. c. A golden lampstand

15. True

16. temple, full

17. response, authentic

18. temple, receive

19. "And, behold, the glory of the God of Israel came from the way of the east: and his voice was like a noise of many waters: and the earth shined with his glory" (Ezekiel 43:2, KJV).

20. Answers will vary.

ANSWER KEY TO LESSON 10

1. Horns: projections from the altar

2. Bullock: a young bull or steer

3. Altar: a place where sacrifices can be made

4. Sin offering: an expiatory sacrifice to cleanse from sin

5. Cubit: length of an elbow to the tip of the middle finger

6. Bottom: sump to catch sacrificial blood

7. Settle: place where the priests would stand and assist the high priest

8. Zadok: joint high priest during David's reign and high priest during the reign of Solomon

9. Handbreadth: distance between index finger to middle finger

10. Purge: make atonement, expiate, forgive, reconcile

11. God speaking directly into her life

12. personal, renewing

13. instructions (or dimensions)

14. e. All of the above

15. d. Bullock

16. heavenly, East

17. precise

18. consecrated, pure

19. "And he said unto me, Son of man, thus saith the Lord GOD; These are the ordinances of the altar in the day when they shall make it, to

offer burnt offerings thereon, and to sprinkle the blood thereon" (Ezekiel 43:18, KJV).

20. Answers will vary.

ANSWER KEY TO LESSON 11

1. Ezekiel: a prophet of God while the Israelites were in Babylon

2. House: dwelling temple

3. Loins: waist

4. En Gedi: a town on the western shore of the Dead Sea

5. Engelaim: an uncertain location on the western shore of the Dead Sea

6. Meat: food

7. Sanctuary: the dwelling place for God and His throne

8. The Dead Sea: the lowest, saltiest body of water in the world

9. Miry places: swamps

10. Marishes: small pools of water

11. She felt a sense of peace overwhelm her heart.

12. source, need

13. provides, restoration

14. d. Twenty-two

15. False

16. Jesus, energizing

17. waters, restorative

18. obedience, deeper

19. "Afterward he measured a thousand; and it was a river that I could not pass over: for the waters were risen, waters to swim in, a river that could not be passed over" (Ezekiel 47:5, KJV).

20. Answers will vary.

ANSWER KEY TO LESSON 12

1. Fellowship: association, community, communion, joint participation

2. Inheritance: possession, property, heritage, portion

3. Lebo-Hamath: a city situated on the Orontes river in Syria

4. Kadesh Barnea: the southern boundary of Israel

5. Damascus: ancient trading city, capital of Syria

6. Waters of strife: oasis at Northern Sinai where Moses struck the rock in anger

7. Strangers: foreigners or immigrants who lived in Israel

8. Joseph: father of the two tribes of Ephraim and Manasseh

9. Divide by lot: allocate a portion of land by chance

10. The Great Sea: the Mediterranean Sea

11. Embracing an old friend

12. church, community

13. inheritance

14. d. Western

15. e. Gentiles

16. promise, faithful

17. Israel, distant

18. description, beginning

19. "And ye shall inherit it, one as well as another: concerning the which I lifted up mine hand to give it unto your fathers: and this land shall fall unto you for inheritance" (Ezekiel 47:14, KJV).

20. Answers will vary.

ANSWER KEY TO LESSON 13

1. Uncircumcised: a man whose foreskin was not removed

2. Unclean: bodily or religiously polluted or defiled

3. Watchman: a person who kept guard over a town or a building and watched for oncoming threats

4. Jerusalem: capital of Israel, name means

"foundation of peace"

5. Zion: a mountain near Jerusalem, the people of God

6. Beauty: comeliness or glory

7. Strength: might or power

8. "Made bare his holy arm": God will comfort His people with His strong arm of deliverance and salvation in the eyes of all the nations

9. Reward: rearguard

10. Vessels of the Lord: vessels stolen from the temple by King Nebuchadnezzar or symbol of total worship experience

11. Chaunel rejoiced; Hakim's salvation

12. rejoicing, salvation

13. arouses, comforts

14. e. Both c. and d.

15. c. Twice

16. captivity, Cyrus

17. seventy, waste

18. determines

19. "For ye shall not go out with haste, nor go by flight: For the LORD shall go before you; and the God of Israel will be your reward" (Isaiah 52:12, KJV).

20. Answers will vary.

ANSWER KEY

ANSWER KEY TO LESSON 1

1. Majesty: greatness, majesty, another name for God
2. Angel: messenger, one who is sent
3. Sin: breaking the law of God
4. Purification rituals: a set of sacrifices and actions designed to make an individual or a group of people holy before God
5. "In these last days": present and end times
6. Worlds: universe, ages or times
7. "Express image of his person": imprint or seal of God's nature
8. "Majesty on high": a title for God, a sign of kingship and authority
9. Purge: to cleanse and wash away sins
10. Ministers: servants and agents of God
11. Poet Laureate
12. Jesus is God, and when He speaks and acts, He is displaying the will of God.
13. Jesus, angels
14. d. Sacrifice an animal for the forgiveness of sins
15. d. Jesus' sacrifice
16. actions, will
17. superior, identity
18. Creator, sustaining
19. "God, who at sundry times and in diverse manners spake in time past unto the fathers by the prophets, Hath in these last days spoken unto us by his Son, whom he hath appointed heir of all things, by whom also he made the worlds" (Hebrews 1:1–2, KJV).
20. Answers will vary.

ANSWER KEY TO LESSON 2

1. Psalms: an instrumental song, a song with words accompanied by musical instruments
2. Thanksgiving: adoration and praise
3. Gods: idols worshiped by other nations and sometimes the Israelite people
4. Pasture: area where sheep could find grass and vegetation to eat freely
5. "Rock of our salvation": name for God
6. Meribah: place where the Israelites sinned against God
7. "Joyful noise": to worship God with joy that compels His people to shout
8. Worship: bowing and submitting to one in authority
9. "Deep places of the earth": bottom of creation
10. Kneel: to bless
11. He was too busy at work because of his promotion.
12. ensure, worship
13. King
14. True
15. e. Both c. and d.
16. worship, heart
17. thanksgiving, psalms of praise
18. jubilation, words
19. "For the LORD is a great God, and a great King above all gods" (Psalm 95:3, KJV).
20. Answers will vary.

ANSWER KEY TO LESSON 3

1. Joy: gladness or happiness; or the object or cause of such

2. Messiah: Christ, Anointed One

3. Shepherds: men who looked after sheep

4. Bethlehem: birthplace of Jesus, city of David

5. Glory: manifestation of God's greatness

6. Bring good tidings: announce, declare good news

7. Saviour: a deliverer, preserver

8. Lord: master

9. Good will: favor

10. Kept: to preserve or conserve something of great importance

11. A baby shower invitation

12. good

13. shepherds, Messiah

14. False

15. d. City of David

16. 70

17. fearful, great

18. poor, outsiders

19. "Glory to God in the highest, and on earth peace, good will toward men" (Luke 2:14, KJV)

20. Answers will vary.

ANSWER KEY TO LESSON 4

1. Gennesaret: triangular coastland on western side of Sea of Galilee

2. "Of little faith": puny, small trust, small burst of belief

3. Sea of Galilee: a sea located north of Jerusalem

4. Hem: fringes or tassels at corner of mantle, which was a Jewish religious requirement

5. Constrained: mentally or physically forced to do something

6. Evening: period before or right after sunset

7. Spirit: phantom or ghost

8. "Be of good cheer": phrase of encouragement and comfort

9. Worship: to fall prostrate in front of the one being worshiped

10. Diseased: physical or mental illness

11. Warren cried out to God and worked hard.

12. ability, impossible

13. impossible, walking

14. North

15. d. Simon

16. seas, sovereign

17. cheer, presence

18. greater, looking

19. "And immediately Jesus stretched forth his hand, and caught him and said unto him, O thou of little faith, wherefore didst thou doubt?" (Matthew 14:31, KJV).

20. Answers will vary.

ANSWER KEY TO LESSON 5

1. "Our Father": the Lord's Prayer, spoken by Jesus at the Last Supper

2. "Hallowed be": to sanctify, to be made holy and pure, venerate

3. Heaven: the abode of God, God's dwelling or resting place

4. Disciples: followers or apprentices

5. Kingdom of God: God's manifested rule on earth as it is in heaven

6. Daily: everyday, appropriate amount for an individual

7. Temptation: trial or test

8. Forgive: send away

9. Importunity: shameless persistence

10. Knock: a persistent effort to see a closed door opened

11. Her mother's calmness

12. relationship, cultivated

13. prays, receives

14. e. Follower

15. d. 46

16. prayer

17. ask, supply

18. impression, created

19. "For every one that asketh receiveth; and he that seeketh findeth; and to him that knocketh it shall be opened" (Luke 11:10, KJV).

20. Answers will vary.

ANSWER KEY TO LESSON 6

1. Pray: to ask for something, beseech, desire

2. Glorify: to bring honor, praise, to recognize

3. John: one of the sons of Zebedee, the first to be handpicked by Jesus

4. Name: a title that encompasses a person's entire identity and character

5. Manifested: revealed

6. Sanctified: set apart

7. Sent: ordered to go to an appointed place

8. One: united

9. "Evil one": Satan

10. "Son of perdition": Judas Iscariot

11. She knows someone knows her and cares about her life.

12. disciples, believe

13. unity

14. e. Patmos

15. oneness, accomplishing

16. authenticate, believe

17. together, Trinity

18. protection, disunity

19. "I pray for them: I pray not for the world, but for them which thou hast given me; for they are thine" (John 17:9, KJV).

20. Answers will vary.

ANSWER KEY TO LESSON 7

1. High priest: head or chief clergy who offered sacrifices to God and appeared in the presence of God to make intercession for the people

2. Order: arrangement, regularity, sequence

3. Melchizedek: a mysterious biblical character first referenced in the book of Genesis as the king of Salem and priest of the Most High God

4. Compassion: to act in moderation or control one's emotion

5. Called: selected

6. "In the days of his flesh": Jesus' earthly ministry

7. Feared: the proper attitude of reverence in duty

8. "Being made perfect": the satisfactory completion of Christ's role as high priest

9. "Eternal salvation": eternal life with Christ for those who believe in him

10. Author: cause

11. Remembering her brother Jay's defense of her

12. Elder, High Priest

13. great

14. d. Bread and wine

15. reach, Jewish

16. role, petition

17. once, atonement

18. Melchizedek, king

19. "Let us therefore come boldly unto the throne of grace, that we may obtain mercy, and find grace to help in time of need" (Hebrews 4:16, KJV).

20. Answers will vary.

ANSWER KEY TO LESSON 8

1. Sick: to be weak, feeble, without strength, powerless

2. Fervent: to be operative, to be at work, to put

forth power

3. Elders: Christians who presided over the gatherings

4. Anointing: to be chosen and designated by God for a particular task, marking by a smearing of oil

5. Elias: the Greek spelling of Elijah

6. Afflicted: to suffer misfortune

7. Oil: olive oil

8. "Shall raise him up": restore to physical health

9. Confess: speak out and make public or agree with

10. Faults: deviation from the right path

11. She didn't want to be embarrassed, and she wasn't super spiritual or a preacher.

12. relationship, power

13. answers

14. True

15. Proverbs, wisdom

16. line, produce

17. expect, forgive

18. situation, person

19. "And the prayer of faith shall save the sick, and the Lord shall raise him up; and if he have committed sins, they shall be forgiven him" (James 5:15, KJV).

20. Answers will vary.

ANSWER KEY TO LESSON 9

1. Pulse: everything that is grown from sown seed, including vegetables, fruit, legumes, grains, and bread

2. Eunuch: a castrated man, commonly appointed in ancient Near Eastern courts to be guardians of the women of the court

3. Nebuchadnezzar: the king of Babylonia who conquered Jerusalem

4. Defile: to pollute, stain, or desecrate

5. Melzar: the eunuch in charge of Daniel and

his friends

6. Fasting: denying oneself certain foods (or other commonly enjoyed substances or activities) in order to focus on God

7. Hananiah, Mishael, and Azariah: the Hebrew names of Daniel's friends Shadrach, Mishael, and Abednego

8. Hypocrite: one who acts in contradiction to his or her stated beliefs or feelings

9. Kosher: in accordance with the dietary laws God relates in the Old Testament Law

10. Yom Kippur: the Day of Atonement; a Jewish festival that required fasting

11. denying, relationship

12. hungering after the presence of God

13. Daniel and his friends, see

14. e. All of the above

15. False

16. Hebrew, earth

17. loyal, name

18. kosher

19. "As for these four children, God gave them knowledge and skill in all learning and wisdom: and Daniel had understanding in all visions and dreams" (Daniel 1:17, KJV).

20. Answers will vary.

ANSWER KEY TO LESSON 10

1. Lawyers: scribes who specialized in studying, teaching, and defending the Law of Moses

2. Samaritans: people despised by Jews for being of mixed race: part Jew and part Gentile

3. Compassion: love, empathy, and mercy motivated by the need of another

4. Levite: a descendant of Levi, but not of Aaron, who helped the priests at the temple

5. Neighbor: one who is near; a fellow person or creature

6. Heart, Soul, Strength, Mind: a person's complete being, that with which we are to love

God

7. Priest: a descendant of Aaron who led the religious rituals at the temple in Jerusalem

8. The Shema: a passage in Deuteronomy 6 at the heart of Jewish religion

9. Tested: to put to the test, try, tempt

10. Ubuntu: a Bantu philosophy centered on understanding that personhood is impossible in isolation

11. She brought him a meal.

12. our neighbor

13. priest, Levite, Samaritan

14. religious

15. True

16. test and trap Him

17. b. Question

18. Shema

19. "And he answering said, Thou shalt love the Lord thy God with all thy heart, and with all thy soul, and with all thy strength, and with all thy mind; and thy neighbour as thyself" (Luke 10:27, KJV).

20. Answers will vary.

ANSWER KEY TO LESSON 11

1. Son of Man: a title for Jesus that shows His humanity

2. Mount of Olives: a limestone ridge to the east of Jerusalem where several key biblical events take place

3. Cursed: given over to destruction; judged and punished, rejected by God

4. Inherit: to take possession of

5. Separate: to set a boundary, divide

6. Everlasting fire: the place of punishment for the unrighteous prepared for the devil

7. Olivet Discourse: Matthew 24:4–25:46, where Jesus answers His disciples' questions about the end times

8. Sheep: a symbol for the righteous who helped

those less fortunate

9. Goats: a symbol for the unrighteous who did not love their neighbors

10. Parabolic: relating to parables (moralistic, sometimes allegorical, stories often used in Jesus' teaching)

11. The homeless and poor

12. the Lord Jesus Himself

13. sheep, goats, righteous, unrighteous

14. b. Humanity

15. False

16. d. It is unclear.

17. care

18. charity, Christ Himself

19. "Then shall the King say unto them on his right hand, Come, ye blessed of my Father, inherit the kingdom prepared for you from the foundation of the world" (Matthew 25:34, KJV).

20. Answers will vary.

ANSWER KEY TO LESSON 12

1. Principalities: evil, malicious spirits that oppose God and His people

2. Armor: resources for both offense and defense in battle

3. Breastplate: armor that covers the body from neck to thighs

4. Supplication: a special request or favor sought for some special necessity from God

5. Righteousness: justification, the process whereby God through Christ puts the sinner in the right relationship with Himself

6. Shield: a long, oblong, four-cornered shield covering the whole body

7. Mystery of the Gospel: Paul's message that through Christ there is free, full salvation for everyone who comes in faith

8. Epistle: a letter

9. Spiritual warfare: battles fought not physically,

but in our spirits against the forces that oppose God

10. Satan: the chief devil and enemy of God

11. Because Clarence was a Christian, but Dave was an atheist.

12. equips

13. b. The sword of the Spirit and the breastplate of righteousness

14. fallen angels

15. True

16. battle; military

17. ourselves; brother and sisters

18. b. Affection

19. "For we wrestle not against flesh and blood, but against principalities, against powers, against the rulers of the darkness of this world, against spiritual wickedness in high places" (Ephesians 6:12, KJV).

20. Answers will vary.

ANSWER KEY

ANSWER KEY TO LESSON 1

1. Perea: a large region east of the Jordan River, northeast of Jerusalem, where John the Baptist did most of his ministry

2. Baptism: a common Jewish cleansing ritual that showed purity or membership

3. Jordan River: a river marking the traditional eastern boundary of the Promised Land, where John the Baptist did his baptizing

4. Dove: symbol of peace and the Holy Spirit

5. Taketh away: bear away, carry off

6. John the Baptist: the son of Zacharias and Elisabeth; a prophet who preached the imminent coming of the kingdom of God; the forerunner of Jesus Christ

7. Zacharias and Elisabeth: John the Baptist's elderly parents; both were righteous people from the tribe of Levi

8. Lamb of God: title for Jesus that alludes to the Passover lamb

9. Passover: Jewish festival that included the sacrifice of a lamb as a remembrance of God's protection of His people in Egypt

10. Manifest: to appear as one truly is

11. He was more confident and bold, shared Christ with others, and blessed other men in the church.

12. Spirit

13. False

14. Perea, Jordan, Jerusalem

15. d. Jewish

16. camel, locusts and honey

17. c. Cousins

18. True

19. "This is he of whom I said, After me cometh a man which is preferred before me: for he was before me" (John 1:30, KJV).

20. Answers will vary.

ANSWER KEY TO LESSON 2

1. Fatherless: orphans, who in biblical days were particularly vulnerable because they did not have any family to provide or advocate for them

2. Comforter: one who is called to one's side, especially called to one's aid

3. Motif: a persistent theme, like love in John's Gospel

4. Iscariot: a kind of surname for the disciple Judas who betrayed Jesus that distinguishes him from the other Judas of the Twelve

5. Upper Room: the place where Jesus and His disciples had the Passover meal before Jesus was betrayed, where Jesus gave the Twelve some teachings about love and the Holy Spirit

6. Third Person of the Trinity: the Holy Spirit of God who comforts and enlightens the believer

7. Commandment: an order, charge, precept, or injunction

8. Advocate: one of the ways to translate a title for the Holy Spirit that reflects how the Spirit pleads our case

9. Comfortless: desolate, helpless, fatherless

10. "The world": the unbelievers, especially those who did not receive the Spirit of truth and to whom Jesus has not manifest Himself

11. To tell his wife that he still appreciated and loved her.

12. empowers, guidance

13. The Holy Spirit would help them.

14. provide, court

15. b. God spared their firstborn children from the tenth plague in Egypt

16. surprised, confused

17. natural

18. a. Teacher

19. "If ye love me, keep my commandments" (John 14:15, KJV).

20. Answers will vary.

ANSWER KEY TO LESSON 3

1. Expedient: profitable, beneficial, for one's good

2. Reprove: to correct or criticize someone with the purpose of convincing him or her of sin or wrongdoing

3. Zebedee: the father of the disciples James and John; a fisherman

4. "Prince of this world": Satan, the devil

5. Judgment: decision, passing a verdict by a jury or a tribunal

6. Spirit of Truth: a title for the Holy Spirit that speaks of His work guiding the believer into all the truth about Christ

7. The Father: a name for the first Person of the Trinity who resides in heaven and sent Jesus and the Holy Spirit to earth

8. Legalism: a fault of Jewish religious leaders throughout the Gospel of John that blinds them to the truth

9. Conscience: the Holy Spirit's internal work of convicting people of sin, one small part of His continuing actions

10. Ascension: Jesus' return to heaven after which the Holy Spirit would come

11. older women

12. disciples

13. Sin, righteousness, and judgment

14. altar, temple

15. True

16. John 20:31

17. b. Convict unbelievers and guide believers

18. expedient/profitable, convicting

19. "He shall glorify me: for he shall receive of mine, and shall shew it unto you" (John 16:14, KJV).

20. Answers will vary.

ANSWER KEY TO LESSON 4

1. The Resurrection: Jesus' return from the dead, demonstrating God's power and Christ's deity

2. "The Jews": Jewish religious leaders who opposed Jesus' teaching

3. Pentecost: a Jewish festival 50 days after the Passover, when the Holy Spirit came to the Church

4. Shalom: a common Jewish greeting meaning "Peace be unto you"

5. Remit: to dismiss, forsake, or leave; to forgive debts or sins

6. Retain: to hold onto, not remit, or seize control of

7. Nicodemus: a Pharisee who listened to Jesus

8. Mary Magdalene: a follower of Jesus who was the first to see Him after the Resurrection

9. Show: to give evidence or proof of a thing

10. Send: either to order someone to go with a connotation of authority, or simply to order or thrust someone to go out

11. By creating an organization that gives young women the same kind of help that Joy gave Ama.

12. God's glory

13. c. Peace be unto you

14. False

15. leaders

16. King, Romans

17. d. All the above.

18. Pentecost

19. "Then said Jesus to them again, Peace be unto you: as my Father hath sent me, even so send I you" (John 20:21, KJV).

20. Answers will vary.

ANSWER KEY TO LESSON 5

1. Victory processions: parades given in honor of winning a significant war, given for generals, soldiers, or kings

2. Palm tree: an ancient symbol of victory

3. Gospel of Mark: the story of Jesus written between A.D. 66 and 70 in Rome reaffirming the Messiah's true mission

4. Bethphage: a village just outside of Jerusalem, a Sabbath day's journey away from it

5. Bethany: a village just outside of Jerusalem, where Jesus spent the night after His Triumphal Entry

6. Hosanna: a shout of praise meaning "Save us now!"

7. Feast of Tabernacles: a Jewish festival commemorating the harvest and the time God provided for His people in the wilderness

8. Colt: a young equine, such as a donkey or horse

9. Sabbath day's journey: a measure of about 1,000 yards, which was the farthest a Jew could travel on the Sabbath without it being considered work

10. Hallel: a Hebrew word meaning "praise"; the praise Psalms 113–118

11. Her mother

12. honor

13. Bethany

14. True

15. suffer, die, rise again

16. Jerusalem

17. b. Suffering Servant

18. generals

19. "Blessed be the kingdom of our father David, that cometh in the name of the Lord: Hosanna in the highest" (Mark 11:10, KJV).

20. Answers will vary.

ANSWER KEY TO LESSON 6

1. Gospel: "Good news," a word used to announce God's grace and His coming kingdom

2. Paul: an apostle called to witness to the Gentiles

3. Apostolic: related to the apostles like Peter, the Twelve, or Paul

4. Eschatological: related to the end times

5. Firstfruits: the best produce, picked first at harvest and usually offered to God

6. Cephas: another form of Peter's name

7. Adam: the first man, through whom sin entered into humanity

8. "Fallen asleep": a common euphemism for death

9. James: Jesus' half-brother, a major leader in the church at Jerusalem who saw Jesus after His resurrection

10. The Twelve: Jesus' disciples

11. mother

12. resurrection

13. d. Pontius Pilate

14. Augustus Caesar

15. True

16. a. Giving to the Jerusalem church

17. died, was buried, rose again

18. Scripture, apostolic

19. "For since by man came death, by man came also the resurrection of the dead" (1 Corinthians 15:21, KJV).

20. Answers will vary.

ANSWER KEY TO LESSON 7

1. Cain: the eldest son of Adam and Eve, who killed his brother Abel

2. Agape: a Greek word for love; in the New Testament, unconditional, divine love

3. Truth: right as pertaining to God and the duties of man, morality, and religion

4. The Wicked One: one who is bad or would cause harm; Satan

5. Bowels: the intestines, considered to be the seat of emotion; so figuratively tender mercy or inward affection

6. John (the Apostle): one of Jesus' closest disciples, the author of the last Gospel and three epistles

7. Abide: to continually be present; to remain, last, or endure

8. Narcissistic: self-centered and self-loving

9. Perceive: to obtain knowledge especially by looking

10. Condemn: to find fault, blame, or accuse

11. She gave it to Candice so she could go on the class trip.

12. words; taking action

13. b. deed and truth

14. tiller, keeper

15. each other

16. natural result, pre-condition

17. d. Expressing the love of God

18. False

19. "Hereby perceive we the love of God, because he laid down his life for us: and we ought to lay down our lives for the brethren" (1 John 3:16, KJV).

20. Answers will vary.

ANSWER KEY TO LESSON 8

1. Day of Judgment: the final, ultimate judgment of God on all humanity

2. Johannine: related to the apostle John

3. Grievous: heavy, important, savage, and fierce

4. Fear: the antithesis of love

5. Overcome: to conquer, prevail, or gain victory

6. Confession: an intellectual acknowledgement and personal acceptance

7. Perfect: to complete or accomplish a goal, maturity

8. Torment: the fear and punishment of judgment

9. Believe: to trust, have personal faith in and personal union with someone

10. Boldness: confidence, the absence of fear

11. She simply talked to him and related her own discomfort.

12. visible, invisible

13. b. Fear

14. John, 1 John, 2 John, 3 John

15. False

16. love

17. direct correlation

18. d. All of the above.

19. "For this is the love of God, that we keep his commandments: and his commandments are not grievous" (1 John 5:3, KJV).

20. Answers will vary.

ANSWER KEY TO LESSON 9

1. Chosen Lady: the addressee of 2 John, a matron living in Asia Minor or else the church itself

2. Elder: an office of the church that exercised leadership and judicial functions in both religious and secular spheres

3. "Walking in truth": the belief and behavior to habitually practice right doctrine and ethics

4. Deceiver: an imposter or misleader; seducer

5. Transgress: to overstep or outstep a bound, to lead before

6. Doctrine: the teaching of Christ

7. God speed: a translation for "rejoice" or "be

glad," a common salutation wishing someone well

8. Beseech: to ask, beg, appeal, or entreat an personal request

9. Docetist: an early Christian heretical sect that thought Jesus' physical form was not real

10. Antichrist: an opponent of the Messiah

11. Because Ron didn't have his beliefs together at all.

12. truth, love

13. c. That we love one another

14. Asia Minor

15. True

16. False

17. b. Final departure from the faith

18. believe, brotherly love

19. "And this is love, that we walk after his commandments. This is the commandment, That, as ye have heard from the beginning, ye should walk in it" (2 John 6, KJV).

20. Answers will vary.

ANSWER KEY TO LESSON 10

1. Gentiles: non-believers, or specifically non-Jews

2. Gaius: a Christian in Asia Minor highly commended by John

3. Fellowhelpers: companions in work, fellow workers

4. Prosper: grant a successful journey, lead by a direct and easy way

5. Truth: dependability, reliability, moral or religious truth

6. Diotrephes: a leader in the church who refused hospitality to Christian workers

7. "Bring forward": to be provided with necessities and escorts for the next stage of the journey

8. Follow: model, imitate, emulate

9. "For His name's sake": a common Hebrew

reference for God

10. Preeminence: the desire to be first

11. They burst into uncontrollable laughter.

12. hospitality

13. c. Truth

14. bishop

15. False

16. spiritual, physical

17. disastrous

18. c. A greeting/general well wishes

19. "I have no greater joy than to hear that my children walk in truth" (3 John 4, KJV).

20. Answers will vary.

ANSWER KEY TO LESSON 11

1. Administrations: service or office, ministering, especially those who faithfully execute commands

2. Operations: activity, experience

3. Idols: anything that is worshiped other than God

4. Ignorant: lack of understanding that leads to error or sin through a mistake

5. Spiritual gifts: special abilities God gives His people to serve the church

6. Knowledge: general items in relation to spiritual things

7. Wisdom: knowledge of the best things to do according to God's will

8. Miracles: demonstrations of power as evidence of the present Messianic age

9. Tongues: unknown languages

10. Lord: title given to Yahweh by Jews, God-fearers, and Christians alike

11. Deacon Ron's words about serving the body

12. contribute

13. c. Cooking

14. idolatry

15. True

16. immorality, unethical

17. different, serve

18. d. Accursed be Jesus

19. "Now concerning spiritual gifts, brethren, I would not have you ignorant" (1 Corinthians 12:1, KJV).

20. Answers will vary.

ANSWER KEY TO LESSON 12

1. Tempered: mixed together, commingled, united one thing to another

2. Schism: a rent, division, or dissension

3. Helps: special ability to aid, assist, and support others

4. Governments: special ability to organize and make decisions that lead to the church operating efficiently and effectively

5. Apostle: one who is sent

6. "Covet earnestly": burn with zeal

7. Comeliness: elegance of figure, gracefulness, and attractiveness

8. Suffer: to experience something in a positive or negative sense

9. Feeble: weak and least powerful

10. Excellent: throwing beyond, beyond measure

11. Nobody asked her to join the choir.

12. part, body

13. c. Schism

14. assist

15. False

16. contributes, functioning

17. rhetorical

18. c. Covet them earnestly

19. "But covet earnestly the best gifts: and yet I shew unto you a more excellent way" (1 Corinthians 12:31, KJV).

20. Answers will vary.

ANSWER KEY TO LESSON 13

1. Utterance: to speak out, speak forth, pronounce

2. Unlearned: one who is unskilled in a particular art, knowledge, profession, or craft; a layman and not a religious official

3. Tongues: ability to speak in a known or unknown language

4. Pentecost: agricultural celebration consisting of thanking God for the firstfruits of the harvest

5. "Was fully come": in the process of fulfillment or coming to an end

6. Confounded: to disturb the mind

7. Amazed: to be beside oneself, out of place

8. Unfruitful: to be barren, not yielding what it ought to yield

9. Bless: to speak well of someone or something

10. Ten thousand: largest number in ancient Greek

11. The many people speaking in tongues in the congregation without an interpretation

12. responsibility, clearly

13. c. Five

14. tongues, unknown

15. False

16. prided

17. instructs, pray

18. c. Glossalalia

19. "Yet in the church I had rather speak five words with my understanding, that by my voice I may teach others also, than ten thousand words in an unknown tongue" (1 Corinthians 14:19, KJV).

20. Answers will vary.

ANSWER KEY TO LESSON 14

1. Charity: love, fellowship, affection, benevolence, or specifically divine kindness

2. Hope: expectation, confidence, or what is longed for

3. Corinth: a major trade city located on an isthmus connecting mainland Greece with the Peloponnesian peninsula

4. "Suffereth long": endures patiently the errors, weaknesses, and even meanness of people

5. Vaunteth: brag

6. Perfect: maturity, completeness

7. Glass: mirror

8. Envieth: earnestly covet another's good fortune

9. "Puffed up": snobbish or arrogant

10. Endureth: continue to be present, does not perish or depart

11. The cookies they brought to the door

12. best, seeks

13. d. All of the above

14. Greece

15. False

16. Ephesus

17. destructive

18. d. Charity

19. "Though I speak with the tongues of men and of angels, and have not charity, I am become as sounding brass, and a tinkling cymbal" (1 Corinthians 13:1, KJV).

20. Answers will vary.

ANSWER KEY

ANSWER KEY TO LESSON 1

1. Transgression: willful deviation from, and therefore rebellion against, the path of moral or godly living

2. Despise: to reject, refuse, despise

3. Tekoa: a small village located west of the Dead Sea, ten miles from Jerusalem

4. Slavery: customary practice throughout Ancient Near East in which a person was sold into slavery to repay personal debt or debt to society

5. "For three transgressions and for four": a pattern showing God's patience is at its limit and cannot restrain His punishment on Israel for their wrongdoing

6. Lies: idols, or anything giving false hope

7. Palaces: citadels and strongholds that made up the king's palace

8. Pant: swallow up or trample

9. Profane: desecrating that which belongs to God

10. Righteous: legally or religiously upright

11. He reviewed Kodjo's lease agreement and helped to renegotiate the lease.

12. view, fight

13. d. Both a. and c.

14. Judah

15. False

16. shepherd, figs

17. rejection

18. c. Idolatry

19. "Thus saith the LORD; For three transgressions of Israel, and for four, I will not turn away the punishment thereof; because they sold the righteous for a pair of silver, and the poor for a pair of shoes" (Amos 2:6, KJV).

20. Answers will vary.

ANSWER KEY TO LESSON 2

1. Gracious: to stoop or bend in kindness to an inferior, considerate, to show favor

2. Righteousness: being in the right, justified, just

3. Feast Days: pilgrimage festivals that required the participation from the entire Israelite community

4. Sikkuth: Mesopotamian astral deity

5. Kaiwan: Babylonian Saturn god

6. "The Day of the Lord": when the Lord appears to wage holy war with His enemies

7. Assemblies: solemn gatherings on the seventh day of the Feast of Unleavened Bread and the eighth day of the Feast of Tabernacles

8. Meat offerings: sacrifices devoid of blood intended as gifts to the Lord

9. Burnt offerings: sacrifices in which the whole animal was consumed with fire

10. Stream: desert wadi or narrow valley flooded with rain water

11. Jenna gave the lady a ride to the shop.

12. pursue, oppose

13. d. Both a. and c.

14. feast

15. True

16. idol

17. continual

18. d. All of the above

19. "Seek good, and not evil, that you may live: and so the LORD, the God of hosts, shall be with you, as ye have spoken" (Amos 5:14, KJV).

20. Answers will vary.

ANSWER KEY TO LESSON 3

1. Chant: to improvise carelessly, to stammer

2. Afflict: to squeeze or oppress

3. Viols: instruments similar to harp and lyre

4. Ointments: oils used for medicinal, cosmetic, and religious purposes

5. "Hamath to the river of the wilderness": the entirety of the undivided kingdom of Israel

6. "Excellency of Jacob": city of Samaria, national self-confidence

7. Abhor: to hate

8. Bowls: special bowls or basins for drinking wine

9. Joseph: the Northern Kingdom of Israel

10. Lo Debar: a town in the Transjordan; the name means "not a thing"

11. He ignored her and instructed his driver to keep driving.

12. participate

13. c. Feasting and lounging

14. encompassed

15. False

16. superior

17. increase

18. c. Recaptured

19. "For, behold, the LORD commandeth, and he will smite the great house with breaches, and the little house with clefts" (Amos 6:11, KJV).

20. Answers will vary.

ANSWER KEY TO LESSON 4

1. Sackcloth: rough woven cloth worn in humiliation and mourning

2. End: final judgement; in Hebrew, a homonym with "summer fruit"

3. Amos: a prophet from Judah who ministered in Israel around 750 B.C.

4. New Moon: a festival held at the beginning of every lunar month

5. Summer fruit: fruit that was not preserved but eaten as soon as it was gathered, a sign of Israel's "end"

6. Howling: an inarticulate shattering stream common during funerals

7. "And it shall come to pass": a phrase denoting what follows as occurring in the future

8. "Mourning of an only son": a picture of hopelessness

9. "Make the ephah small and the shekel great": to increase prices by paring down the quantity sold and using uneven balances

10. "Baldness on every head": every person in Israel will be touched by grief causing calamity

11. Why Lakisha wasn't getting paid enough and how she could get such great deals at the store

12. injustice

13. d. Both a. and b.

14. festival

15. True

16. visions

17. symbol

18. b. New Moon and Sabbath

19. "And it shall come to pass in that day, saith the Lord GOD, that I will cause the sun to go down at noon, and I will darken the earth in the clear day" (Amos 8:9, KJV).

20. Answers will vary.

ANSWER KEY TO LESSON 5

1. Parable: a proverb or byword

2. Prophesy: to cause to drip or make words flow

3. Micah: a prophet whose name means "Who is

like Yahweh?"

4. House of Jacob: God's people, all of Israel

5. Lamentation: elegy or dirge

6. Straightened: short of spirit, quick-tempered, impatient

7. Rest: the Promised Land

8. Polluted: to become unclean sexually, religiously, or ceremonially

9. "Cast the cord by lot": to use a cord or measuring line to divide up the land

10. "Men averse from war": innocent and peaceful travelers

11. The thought of being indicted

12. justify

13. a. One to cast the cord by lot

14. Yahweh

15. False

16. description

17. Judah, message

18. c. Mock them

19. "If a man walking in the spirit and falsehood do lie, saying, I will prophesy unto thee of wine and of strong drink; he shall even be the prophet of this people" (Micah 2:11, KJV).

20. Answers will vary.

ANSWER KEY TO LESSON 6

1. Confounded: to be ashamed, embarrassed

2. Equity: upright, straight, level

3. Heads: leaders of families and elders of tribes

4. False prophets: those who comforted the people without pointing out sin or challenging people to repent

5. Err: to wander

6. Bite: vex or oppress

7. Divine: to seek to understand the will of the gods

8. Judgement: establishment of right through fair and legal procedures in accordance with the law and will of God

9. Zion: the hill that David conquered, the temple, or Jerusalem

10. Lean: to lie, rely, or rest on

11. He evaded her questions.

12. abandon

13. c. Power by the spirit of the Lord

14. prophets

15. False

16. Neo-Assyrian

17. build

18. d. Both b. and c.

19. "Then shall the seers be ashamed, and the diviners confounded: yea, they shall all cover their lips; for there is no answer from God" (Micah 3:7, KJV).

20. Answers will vary.

ANSWER KEY TO LESSON 7

1. Redeem: to ransom, rescue, or deliver

2. Mercy: goodness or kindness (especially as extended to the lowly, needy, miserable, or those in a lower position of power)

3. Balaam: ancient Near Eastern prophet who did not serve the Israelite God

4. Human sacrifice: a sacrifice of the firstborn son as the most precious thing to the family

5. Wearied: to be tired or to give up

6. Testify: to answer in a legal suit, to provide opposing testimony

7. Bowing: an act that shows homage or respect to royalty

8. "Fruit of my body": firstborn child

9. Justice: judgment or right sentence

10. Humbly: to act submissively

11. He was led astray from the initial purpose of opening a restaurant.

12. desires

13. c. Perfection

14. regarded

15. False

16. Samaria, Jerusalem

17. heart

18. b. Shittim and Gilgal

19. "For I brought thee up out of the land of Egypt, and redeemed thee out of the house of servants; and I sent before thee Moses, Aaron, and Miriam" (Micah 6:4, KJV).

20. Answers will vary.

ANSWER KEY TO LESSON 8

1. Remnant: the rest, what is left, remaining descendants

2. Iniquity: perversity or guilt

3. Bashan: an area east of the Jordan river

4. Gilead: area next to Bashan known for its healing balm

5. Rod: a stick used by shepherds to control sheep

6. "Lick the dust like a serpent": to be humiliated, or perhaps to die in defeat

7. Compassion: tender maternal love

8. "Dwell solitarily in the woods": not living in a good situation

9. Delighteth: take pleasure in

10. Pardoneth: lift, carry, raise, or take away

11. Lane allowing the builder to explain

12. consequences, necessary

13. d. Both b. and c.

14. Bashan

15. True

16. lamenting

17. rejoices

18. c. When they came out of Egypt

19. "He will turn again, he will have compassion on us; he will subdue our iniquities; and thou wilt cast all their sins into the depths of the sea" (Micah 7:19, KJV).

20. Answers will vary.

ANSWER KEY TO LESSON 9

1. Recompense: punishment or reward for an action, benefit

2. Intercessor: one who intervenes or interposes oneself

3. Islands: Mediterranean coastline or maritime region

4. Redeemer: one who buys property back into the family; an avenger of blood; God as He reestablishes relationship

5. Fear: godly, reverent, childlike fear from the acknowledgment of God's name

6. Arm: dynamic metaphor for the saving action of God

7. Sustain: support

8. Cloak: outer garment worn by men of rank and high priest

9. Fury: heat or venom of a snake

10. Zeal: passionate, ardent love of God toward His people

11. The human resources manager had mistreated him.

12. partner

13. c. Sword

14. represent

15. True

16. Assyrian

17. oppose

18. c. Like a pent-up flood

19. "And he saw that there was no man, and wondered that there was no intercessor: therefore his own arm brought salvation for him; and his righteousness, it sustained him" (Isaiah 59:16, KJV).

20. Answers will vary.

ANSWER KEY TO LESSON 10

1. Amend: to reform, make well or right

2. Abominations: idolatrous practices, various kinds of wickedness

3. Shiloh: place in Northern Israel where the tabernacle resided from the time of Judges until the Philistines captured it

4. Temple in Jerusalem: the magnificent temple Solomon built

5. Trust: to feel safe or confident in

6. "The land": the land promised to the Israelites

7. "Thoroughly execute judgment": truly or really execute judgment

8. Delivered: to take away or snatch away, e.g., from violence

9. Den: hideout

10. "Rising up early": earnestness

11. Jeff asked God to change his heart.

12. actions, amend

13. d. The temple

14. tabernacle

15. True

16. Babylonians

17. faith

18. c. A den of robbers

19. "Behold, ye trust in lying words, that cannot profit" (Jeremiah 7:8, KJV).

20. Answers will vary.

ANSWER KEY TO LESSON 11

1. Soul: life, creature, the inner being of a person

2. Turn: to turn back or turn away from evil

3. Proverbs: a way of summarizing wisdom or real life truth

4. Usury: the act of giving a loan with exorbitant interest

5. Fathers: head or founder of a household, group, or clan

6. Heart: mind or inclination

7. "Sour grapes": image from a proverb referring to the sins of the fathers

8. Spirit: breath, mental, and spiritual essence of the human or divine

9. Pleasure: to delight or take joy in

10. Live: to restore to life or quicken

11. Dealing drugs

12. responsibility

13. d. Sour grapes

14. summarizing

15. False

16. Babylonia

17. responsible

18. a. The death of him that dieth

19. "Behold, all souls are mine; as the soul of the father, so also the soul of the son is mine: the soul that sinneth, it shall die" (Ezekiel 18:4, KJV).

20. Answers will vary.

ANSWER KEY TO LESSON 12

1. Wrath: Great anger or fierce rage

2. Desolate: laid waste, uninhabited, or deserted

3. Zechariah: a prophet, the son of Berechiah

4. Post-Exilic Period: the time of Israel's history after the returning of the exiles to Jerusalem in 538 b.c.

5. Whirlwind: the result of two currents from opposite directions combining to create a circular motion of wind

6. Oppress: defraud from a position of power

7. Hearken: to listen and obey

8. Adamant stone: hard point of a stylus, usually made out of quartz

9. Mercy and Compassions: the natural response and outgrowth of the mercy the people received from the Lord's hand.

10. Stopped their ears: made their ears heavy

11. John could trust where the food came from

and the quality of the food. Plus the workers were paid a livable wage

3:6, KJV).

20. Answers will vary.

12. overnight, hearing

13. c. whirlwind

14. boy

15. True

16. Persian

17. Past

18. c. Turn your back

19. But they refused to hearken, and pulled away the shoulder, and stopped their ears, that they should not hear.

20. Answers will vary

ANSWER KEY TO LESSON 13

1. Purge: purify, distill, strain, refine

2. Ordinance: civil enactment prescribed by God, a prescribed limit

3. Refiner: those who would purify or refine precious metal

4. Fuller: someone who cleaned clothes

5. Hireling: hired servant

6. Tithes and offerings: a tenth of one's possessions offered to God and obligatory sacrifices

7. Prepare: to remove, to clear a path

8. Abide: survive or endure

9. Soap: lye or potash

10. Curse: to condemn or call down judgment on

11. He worked hard for his money.

12. just

13. c. Sit as a refiner

14. crucible, bellows

15. False

16. post-exilic

17. robbed

18. c. Return to them

19. "For I am the LORD, I change not; therefore ye sons of Jacob are not consumed" (Malachi

NOTES

NOTES

NOTES

NOTES

NOTES

NOTES

NOTES

NOTES

NOTES

NOTES